About the Marine Sanctuaries Conservation Series

The National Oceanic and Atmospheric Administration's Marine Sanctuary Division (MSD) administers the National Marine Sanctuary Program. Its mission is to identify, designate, protect and manage the ecological, recreational, research, educational, historical, and aesthetic resources and qualities of nationally significant coastal and marine areas. The existing marine sanctuaries differ widely in their natural and historical resources, and include nearshore and open ocean areas ranging in size from less than one to over 5,000 square miles. Protected habitats include rocky coasts, kelp forests, coral reefs, sea grass beds, estuarine habitats, hard and soft bottom habitats, segments of whale migration routes, and shipwrecks.

Because of considerable differences in settings, resources, and threats, each marine sanctuary has a tailored management plan. Conservation, education, research, monitoring and enforcement programs vary accordingly. Fundamental to marine protected area management is the integration of these programs. The Marine Sanctuaries Conservation Series reflects and supports this integration by providing a forum for publication and discussion of the complex issues currently facing the National Marine Sanctuary Program. Topics of published reports vary substantially, and may include descriptions of educational programs, discussions on resource management issues, and summaries of scientific research and monitoring projects. The series will facilitate integration of natural sciences, socioeconomic and cultural sciences, education, and policy development to accomplish the diverse needs of NOAA's resource protection mandate.

The Economic Contribution of Whalewatching to Regional Economies:
Perspectives From Two National Marine Sanctuaries

Foreword

Brad Barr
Senior Program Analyst
National Marine Sanctuary Program

I

**Valuing Hawai`i's Humpback Whales:
The Economic Impact of Humpbacks on
Hawai`i's Ocean Tour Boat Industry**

Dan Utech
Hawaiian Islands Humpback Whale National Marine Sanctuary

II

The Demand for Whalewatching at Stellwagen Bank National Marine Sanctuary

Porter Hoagland and Andrew E. Meeks
Marine Policy Center
Woods Hole Oceanographic Institution

U. S. Department of Commerce
William M. Daley, Secretary

National Oceanic and Atmospheric Administration
D. James Baker, Under Secretary

National Ocean Service
Nancy Foster, Assistant Administrator

Silver Spring, Maryland
July 2000

DISCLAIMER

Report content does not necessarily reflect the views and policies of the National Marine Sanctuary Program or the National Oceanic and Atmospheric Administration, nor does the mention of trade names or commercial products constitute endorsement or recommendation for use.

REPORT AVAILABILITY

Electronic copies of this report may be downloaded from the National Marine Sanctuaries Program web site at www.sanctuaries.nos.noaa.gov. Hard copies may be available from the following address:

National Oceanic and Atmospheric Administration
Marine Sanctuaries Division
SSMC4, N/ORM62
1305 East-West Highway
Silver Spring, MD 20910

SUGGESTED CITATIONS

Utech, D. 2000. "Valuing Hawai`i's Humpback Whales: The Economic Impact of Humpbacks on Hawai`i's Ocean Tour Boat Industry." In: *The Economic Contribution of Whalewatching to Regional Economies: Perspectives From Two National Marine Sanctuaries*. Marine Sanctuaries Conservation Series MSD-00-2. U.S. Department of Commerce, National Oceanic and Atmospheric Administration, Marine Sanctuaries Division, Silver Spring, MD.

Hoagland, P. and A.E. Meeks. 2000. "The Demand for Whalewatching at Stellwagen Bank National Marine Sanctuary." In: *The Economic Contribution of Whalewatching to Regional Economies: Perspectives From Two National Marine Sanctuaries*. Marine Sanctuaries Conservation Series MSD-00-2. U.S. Department of Commerce, National Oceanic and Atmospheric Administration, Marine Sanctuaries Division, Silver Spring, MD.

TABLE OF CONTENTS

FOREWORD

Brad Barr
Senior Program Analyst
National Marine Sanctuary Program

Whenever human beings have looked out on the sea, they have seen whales. First from the shore and later from ships when humanity entered the ocean realm as seafarers, we have responded to seeing these creatures with awe and wonder. Even when we hunted whales, a period well chronicled both in history and in literature, the sight of a whale brought an adrenaline rush that was not totally linked to potential economic gain. The first trips on boats specifically to watch, rather than hunt, whales began around 45 years ago in Southern California where the migrating gray whales, seen in the distance from land, drew vessels out for a closer look. Since that time whalewatching has boomed, currently conducted in over 40 countries around the world, including Antarctica, and estimated by economists at the Whale and Dolphin Conservation Society to have a 1999 worldwide economic value of around $800 million USD. The economic contribution to local coastal communities is particularly significant in developing countries and those where declining fish populations (and in some cases like the Japanese, international bans on whaling) have driven harvesters to look for viable alternatives. Clearly, whalewatching is now, in many places around the world, a small but thriving part of the regional economy. Like in the days of whaling, we still get the rush, but for some, money is back contributing to the physiological response.

The experience of whalewatching is essentially the same everywhere. While a small amount of whalewatching is conducted from land, most is done from boats. These can be small boats, such as the rigid-bottom inflatables used for orca tours in the Pacific Northwest, looking at the humpbacks in Hawaii, or the belugas and blue whales in the Gulf of St. Lawrence off the Saguenay River in Quebec. They can also be large boats, most recently high speed catamarans that take 100-200 or more whalewatchers to the prime New England whale grounds or off the Australian coast in places like Hervey Bay. Most are day-trip boats, but they can also be cruise ships, like the ones that visit the feeding humpbacks and orcas in Glacier Bay, Alaska each summer. The dayboat trips are generally for half or a full day, depending on the distance to the whale grounds and the cruising speed of the vessel, and most have a naturalist or whale expert aboard to help interpret what is seen on the trip, and to educate passengers on whale natural history and conservation. Whalewatching can be conducted as a directed activity, where the focus of the trip is watching whales, or it can be something that is opportunistic, where it may happen if whales are encountered (such as a snorkel trip in Hawaii where whales may be seen on the trip to and from the reefs, or even the gambling ships that head to the international waters off New England that include the possibility of seeing whales in their advertising).

The National Marine Sanctuary Program has been significantly affected by the growth of the whalewatching industry. Some sort of directed whalewatching occurs at most of the sites, with whale grounds at Stellwagen and Hawaii alone hosting more than 1.2 million visitors a year. For these sites, and for many of the other sanctuaries, whalewatching represents one of the most important uses of the sanctuary waters, and can present some significant challenges.

No sanctuary in the system currently has specific regulations regarding whalewatching. While the vessels and captains are subject to general passenger vessel safety requirements, there are few if any Federal regulations beyond minimum approach distance regulations, that apply to all vessels, for humpbacks in Hawaii and Northern right whales on the East Coast. One of the reasons why there are few regulations for whalewatching is that the majority of scientists and managers who work with marine mammals believe that whalewatching is not inherently damaging to whales. The prevailing thinking about whalewatching is that the opportunity to educate and inform passengers about whales and conservation issues more than balances what little harassment-related impacts there might be to individual animals. While there have been few, if any, scientific studies that conclusively demonstrate that whalewatching is benign, all the scientific literature and studies of populations of whales in areas where significant whalewatching occurs, taken together, seems to suggest that populations in those areas have exhibited no real symptoms of being adversely affected by this activity. However, as the number of vessels engaged in whalewatching, and the cruising speeds of those vessels, increase, whalewatch vessels have collided with whales, causing serious injuries and in a few cases, have killed the whales struck. These ship strikes pose a risk to whales in areas where many fast whalewatch vessels operate, and steps are being taken to address this problem. In the US and Canada, resource managers, scientists, and the industry are meeting to collaboratively develop and implement voluntary operational guideline or codes of conduct to reduce the likelihood of striking or wounding any more whales. Given the uncertainty with regard to adverse impacts associated with harassment, and therefore the need to act in a precautionary way in the absence of certainty, such guidelines will also have the effect of helping to mitigate any unanticipated impacts to individuals resulting from whalewatch operations. If whales continue to be struck and killed after these guidelines have been implemented, the issue of regulations may have to be revisited.

One of the important aspects of the National Marine Sanctuary Program is that unlike areas set aside strictly for preservation, Sanctuaries are areas where some human activities, even ones involving commercial extraction of resources, can be allowed to continue after a site is designated so long as they don't adversely affect the nationally significant resources of the site. This is a very difficult balance to achieve, perhaps far more difficult than preservation which may simply involve closing off an area to most uses and providing an effective enforcement program to insure that the restrictions are complied with by any user that might be allowed inside. It is very much like what happens in a National Forest, where nationally significant forest areas are being protected, but carefully managed logging is allowed. In order to make informed decisions regarding the fate of these existing uses, Sanctuary Managers must have the best, most scientifically robust information available about those resources. Biological, chemical, and physical oceanography of the site, life history information, and ecological interactions are all important but equally so is the social and economic value of that activity. The following two studies were commissioned by the National Marine Sanctuary Program elements at the Studds/Stellwagen Bank NMS and the Hawaiian Islands Humpback Whale NMS to assist Sanctuary Managers in understanding the economics of the whalewatch industry in these regions. They have been conducted using entirely different analytical methodologies, but both provide rigorous scientific analyses of whalewatch economics, information essential to the effective management of our national marine sanctuaries.

The first paper is a study conducted by Dan Utech, who at the time was a Presidential Management Intern working at the Hawaiian Islands Humpback Whale National Marine Sanctuary (HIHWNMS). Like the authors of the second work, the basis for this analysis is an intensive survey, but in this case integrating this new data to establish 1999 direct revenue estimates from survey data, and extrapolating indirect and induced revenues and jobs supported through an Input-Output model used in 1992 by the State of Hawaii to estimate the overall value of the State's ocean tour industry. It is somewhat more comprehensive than the second study, including activities where whalewatching is not the only activity being conducted on these boat trips, but also provides another scientifically rigorous estimate of the economic value of whalewatching in the Hawaiian Sanctuary.

The second paper was a study conducted by Porter Hoagland and Andy Meeks from the Marine Policy Center at the Woods Hole Oceanographic Institution in Woods Hole, Massachusetts, for the Studds/Stellwagen Bank National Marine Sanctuary. Completed in 1997, with recent revisions for this publication, this study calculated the economic value of whalewatching at SSBNMS, where over 90% of the New England regional whalewatching effort is directed. The authors conducted an intensive survey of the whalewatch operators during the July and August 1996 whalewatching season, using an traditional economic analytical tool called "zonal travel cost methodology," selected because it is simple, requires limited data, and is widely accepted by economists for this type of application. From this analysis, the authors were able to provide reasonably rigorous, conservative estimates of the economic value of whalewatching activity in the Sanctuary.

While they do not represent the definitive work on whalewatch economics in the National Marine Sanctuary Program, both of these studies are full of useful and interesting information about this important system-wide activity. In keeping with the Program's focus on getting the most out of each dollar appropriated to it, these two studies were completed for the somewhat remarkable sum of less than $10,000: quality at a reasonable cost. While there is still much to be done to fully understand whalewatching as it is currently conducted in the national marine sanctuaries, this summary document represents a pretty good starting point.

I
Valuing Hawai`i's Humpback Whales:
The Economic Impact of Humpbacks on
Hawai`i's Ocean Tour Boat Industry

Dan Utech
Hawaiian Islands Humpback Whale National Marine Sanctuary

ACKNOWLEDGEMENTS

This report would not have been possible without the valuable assistance of many people. Special thanks go to Dick Poirier, Craig MacDonald, and Jim Coon for their interest, support and input at the design stages of the study. Many tour boat operators took the time to complete the study survey, providing the raw data for the study. A number of ocean tour operators went beyond the surveys to provide additional information about the whale watch and ocean tour boat industry; Maggie Bell, Geoff Wall, Bruce DeYoung, Ronnie Glover, David Jung, Phil Kasper, Mike Dennis and Jim Coon deserve thanks in this regard. In addition, many government and non-governmental representatives provided background information and assisted with the study design, most notably Mike Hamnett, Athlene Clark, Victor Honda, Emily Gardner, Mike Markrich, Xijun Tian, Terry White, and Cathryn Poff. Finally, the staff of the Hawaiian Islands Humpback Whale National Marine Sanctuary—Allen Tom, Claire Cappelle, Cindy Hylkema, Joylinn Oliveira, Naomi MacIntosh, Kellie Araki, Carol Carey, and Jean Souza—helped in every imaginable way.

TABLE OF CONTENTS

LIST OF TABLES

EXECUTIVE SUMMARY

Humpback whales make a major contribution to Hawai`i's economy. One of the primary avenues for this contribution is the ocean tour boat industry. This report quantifies the economic impact of commercial whale watching and other humpback-related ocean touring in Hawai`i. It also quantifies the broader economic impact of the ocean tour boat industry. The estimates are based on a survey of ocean tour boat operators and passengers that was conducted February to July of 1999. The key findings of the study are summarized below.

Whale Watching is a Vital Component of Hawai`i's Ocean Recreation Industry

- A total of 52 vessels offered whale watching trips during the 1999 whale season, and these vessels ran an average total of 87 trips each day.[1] These vessels took approximately 3,100 passengers whale watching per day in Hawai`i during the 1999 whale season; for the 1999 season, the total number of whale watchers was nearly 370,000. Maui is the heart of the whale watching industry, accounting for approximately two-thirds of Hawai`i's whale watching passengers during the 1999 whale season. (See *Whale Watching Tours* for detailed whale watching information).

- Direct revenues attributable to whale watching were $11-16 million in Hawai`i during the 1999 whale season.[2] The low end of this range is an estimate of direct revenues generated by commercial whale watching tours. The upper end of the range is an estimate of the direct revenues from all ocean tour boats that are *attributable* to whale watching; it consists of the $11 million in commercial whale watching direct revenues and a $5 million portion of the direct revenues generated by snorkeling trips. A portion of snorkeling revenues is included based on this study's findings about the importance of whale watching to snorkeling trip passengers. (See *The Role of Humpbacks in the Sale of Other Ocean Tours* for more information on the methodology used to determine the portion of snorkeling revenues to be added to the commercial whale watching revenue base).

- The total economic impact of whale watching in Hawai`i in 1999 was $19-27 million. These figures include direct, indirect and induced revenues.[3] These estimates were generating by

---

[1] For the purposes of this study, the 1999 whale season is defined as December 15, 1998 to April 15, 1999.

[2] The direct revenue estimates in this report include all direct revenues generated by the sale of ocean tours; that is, they include both revenues received by the ocean tour operators themselves and revenues received by middlemen such as activity desks. See Section Appendix A for further information on this topic.

[3] Direct revenues are the dollars spent on ocean tours. does not end with the operators and intermediaries. Indirect revenues are those spent by operators to run their businesses, such as purchasing fuel, food, and snorkeling equipment. Induced revenues are those spent within Hawai`i by employees of operators and intermediaries as a portion of their wages.

using the study's direct revenue estimates in combination with a tourism multiplier from the 1992 Hawai`i State Input-Output Model (Hawai`i Department of Business, Economic Development and Tourism 1998). The low end of the range is the total economic impact of the $11 million of direct commercial whale watching revenues. The upper end of the range is the total economic impact of the $16 million of ocean tour boat revenues attributable to whale watching. (See *The Role of Humpbacks in the Sale of Other Ocean Tours* for more information on the addition of snorkeling revenues to the commercial whale watching revenue base.)

- Commercial whale watching supported the equivalent of 280-390 full-time jobs in Hawai`i in 1999. The jobs estimate was also generated by using a multiplier from the 1992 Hawai`i State Input-Output Model in combination with this study's estimates of 1999 whale watching direct revenues. The lower end of the range reflects the total economic impact of direct whale watching revenues. The lower end of the range is the job impact of the $11 million in direct commercial whale watching revenues. The upper end of the range is the total job impact of the $16 million of ocean tour boat revenues attributable to whale watching. (See *The Role of Humpbacks in the Sale of Other Ocean Tours* for more information on the addition of snorkeling revenues to the whale watching revenue base).

The Broader Ocean Tour Boat Industry Plays a Large, Growing Role in Hawai`i's Economy

Whale watching is only one segment of Hawai`i's multi-faceted ocean tour boat industry. Although the link between humpbacks and the whale watching industry is readily apparent, it was a hypothesis of this study that humpbacks also impact other segments of the tour boat industry. More specifically, it was hypothesized that humpbacks have an impact on three types of ocean tours in addition to whale watching: snorkel tours, dinner cruises, and sunset cruises. In order to test this idea, revenue data were collected for all four of these tour types, which are collectively referred to in this report as the "ocean tour boat industry."[4] In other contexts, this term might be understood to include other ocean tours, such as scuba dives, tourist submarines, and glass bottom boat tours. These were excluded from the scope of this study, however, because humpbacks appeared to be unrelated to them.

To summarize, then, the scope of the study goes beyond whale watching to include snorkel tours, dinner cruises and sunset cruises. This section describes the study's findings about the economic impact of these four ocean tour boat industry segments, without regard to the impact of humpbacks. Due to data limitations, revenues for O`ahu's ocean tour boat industry could not be estimated with this study's data, with the exception of the whale watching segment. Because O`ahu operators are such a large part of the ocean tour boat industry, it was decided to

---

[4] The findings with regard to the impact of humpbacks on snorkeling tours, dinner cruises and sunset cruises is discussed in detail in Section *0*.

update and include a prior estimate of O`ahu's dinner cruise revenues to give a more accurate picture of the state-wide impact of Hawai`i's ocean tour boat industry. [5]

- The 1999 direct revenues from Hawai`i's ocean tour boat industry were approximately $132 million for the full calendar year. See Table 1 for a summary of the revenue estimates. (See *0* and *0* for further details).

- The total economic impact of Hawai`i's ocean tour boat industry is estimated to be $225 million in 1999. This figure includes direct, indirect and induced revenues, and was generated by using the study's direct revenue estimates in combination with a tourism multiplier from the 1992 Hawai`i State Input-Output Model.

- The ocean tour boat industry supported approximately 3,200 jobs in Hawai`i in 1999. This figure includes direct, indirect and induced revenues, and was generated by using the study's direct revenue estimates in combination with a tourism multiplier from the 1992 Hawai`i State Input-Output Model.

- The ocean tour boat industry is a growing segment of Hawai`i's economy. Between 1990 and 1999, total ocean tour boat revenues on the Big Island, Maui and Kaua`i grew by 25 percent in real terms (inflation-adjusted). By contrast, overall visitor expenditures declined slightly in real terms between 1990 and 1998 (1998 being the latest year for which visitor expenditure data are available).

---

[5] The O`ahu dinner cruise revenue estimates included in this study are based on Markrich (1993).

Table 1: Summary of 1999 Economic Impacts of Selected Components of Hawai`i's Ocean Tour Boat Industry (Revenues and Impact in $Millions)

Island	Tour Type	Direct Revenues ($ millions)	Total Economic Impact ($ millions)	Jobs Supported
Big Island	Whale Watching	1.6	2.8	40
	Snorkeling	10.1	17.2	247
	Dinner Cruises	2.1	3.6	52
	Sunset Cruises	1.5	2.5	36
	Big Island Total	15.3	26.1	375
Kaua`i	Whale Watching	0.9	1.6	23
	Snorkeling	17.1	29.3	420
	Dinner Cruises	N/A	N/A	N/A
	Sunset Cruises	3.7	6.4	92
	Kaua`i Total	21.8	37.3	535
Maui	Whale Watching	6.1	10.5	151
	Snorkeling	39.5	67.5	969
	Dinner Cruises	5.1	8.7	125
	Sunset Cruises	1.8	3.1	45
	Maui Total	52.5	89.8	1,290
O`ahu	Whale Watching	2.6	4.4	63
	Snorkeling	N/A	N/A	N/A
	Dinner Cruises	[39.5]	[67.5]	[969]
	Sunset Cruises	N/A	N/A	N/A
	O`ahu Total	42.0	71.9	1,032
Statewide	Whale Watching	11.3	19.3	277
	Snorkeling	66.6	114.0	1,636
	Dinner Cruises	46.7	79.8	1,146
	Sunset Cruises	7.0	12.1	173
	Statewide Total	131.6	225.1	3,232

The O`ahu dinner cruise market estimates are bracketed in Table 1 to show that they are not based on this study's data. As noted above, data limitations precluded estimation of O`ahu ocean tour boat revenues, with the exception of whale watching. To provide a proxy for current O`ahu dinner cruise revenues, a 1990 estimate of O`ahu dinner cruise revenues was adjusted for inflation and included in Table 1. This assumption is believed to be conservative, as it assumes no growth in O`ahu dinner cruise revenues over the 1990-1999 period. Ocean tour boat revenues on the neighbor islands grew over this same period. O'ahu snorkeling tour and sunset cruise revenues are not estimated in this report, and are thus shown as "N/A" in Table 1.

It is important to note that these estimates do not reflect a shift in the dinner cruise market that occurred in April 1999. At that time, a large vessel that had operated dinner cruises on Maui was shifted to Kaua'i. As a result, the estimates presented here underestimate Kaua'i's 1999 dinner cruise revenues (which are thus shown as "N/A" above), and overestimate Maui's 1999 dinner cruise revenues. Nonetheless, the total estimate of dinner cruise revenues across these two islands should not be greatly affected by this change.

As a further point of clarification, it should be noted that the assumptions underlying the direct revenue estimates differ slightly by trip type. For snorkeling tours, dinner cruises and sunset cruises, data collected during the 1999 whale season were used to develop revenue estimates for both the full 1999 calendar year. Whale watching revenue estimates for the 1999 whale season and the full 1999 calendar year, on the other hand, would be nearly identical. The 1999 revenue estimates for the non-whale watching segments are believed to be conservative, in that they are based on data collected during the whale season, and thus do not take the non-whale season trip schedules into account (see Section 0 for further information).

The Economic Impact of Humpbacks and Hawai'i's Ocean Recreation Industry Extends Far Beyond Ocean Tour Revenues

This study's passenger survey provides evidence that Hawai'i's humpback whales are a major factor in some visitors' choice of Hawai'i as a vacation destination. Approximately 75 percent of the Maui dinner cruise and snorkeling tour passengers stated that they knew that humpbacks would be present in Hawaiian waters during their visit. Over 50 percent of ocean tour passengers surveyed indicated that humpbacks were at least a small factor in their decision to come to Hawai'i. Ten percent of visitors surveyed stated that humpbacks were "one of several important factors," and an additional 3 percent described humpbacks as a "very important factor" in their decision to come to Hawai'i.

These data suggest that some of Hawai'i's visitors would vacation elsewhere if the humpbacks were not present in Hawaiian waters. As a result, a full accounting of the economic impact of humpbacks would include all of the tourist expenditures of these visitors. The data collected for this study do not enable a quantitative estimate of this type of impact, but the results do indicate that humpbacks play a role in Hawai'i's tourism market far beyond ocean tour boat industry revenues. In this light, the humpback whale economic impact estimates presented above should be viewed as conservative, in that they focus solely on ocean tour boat revenues.

Key Words: Hawaiian Islands Humpback Whale National Marine Sanctuary, humpback whale, whale-watching, economic value, tourism

14

INTRODUCTION

Two thousand humpback whales—two thirds of the North Pacific stock—migrate to Hawai`i waters each winter. The whales travel from as far away as Alaska, crossing three thousand miles of ocean en route to Hawai`i. Although the reasons for the humpback migration are not known with certainty, scientists believe that Hawai`i's shallow, warm coastal ocean areas provide ideal conditions for birthing, nursing and mating, the primary activities that humpbacks engage in during their stay in Hawai`i. Recognizing the importance of Hawaiian waters to the continued recovery of humpbacks, Congress designated a portion of these waters as the Hawaiian Islands Humpback Whale National Marine Sanctuary in 1992. With the State of Hawai`i's 1997 decision to include state waters in the Sanctuary, the foundation was laid for cooperative protection of 1,370 square miles of ocean for many humpbacks generations to come.

Through the hard work of the Sanctuary and other Hawaiians, humpbacks will have the chance to prosper in the waters of Hawai`i. But the effort is not without its rewards, as humpbacks produce many benefits for Hawai`i's residents and visitors. These magnificent creatures support and stimulate a wide range of economic activity in Hawai`i. Hawai`i's residents and visitors produce and buy art and merchandise that depicts humpbacks. They sponsor and attend festivals in the humpbacks' honor. They produce and consume whale watching tours on Hawai`i's tour boats and shores. And along the way, visitors purchase meals, hotel rooms, and supplies, while residents earn and spend income derived from these activities.

Although all facets of the economic relationship between humpbacks and Hawai`i merit attention, this report focuses on the relationship between humpbacks and Hawai`i's ocean tour industry. This link is the most important, for several reasons. Ocean tours bring thousands of people close to the whales, offering them the opportunity to observe humpbacks in their natural habitat. These close-up encounters engender the widespread interest in humpbacks that creates impacts in other parts of the economy, such as expenditures on whale art and merchandise. At the same time, whale watching and ocean tours generate substantial revenues in their own right. These direct revenues, in turn, generate indirect and induced revenues. Thus, the first step in understanding the economic importance of humpbacks to Hawai`i is an analysis of the link between whales and Hawai`i's ocean tour boat industry.

As a result, the primary aim of this study is to quantify and describe the economic impact of humpbacks on Hawai`i's ocean tour boat industry. More specifically, the study estimates the direct, indirect and induced revenues, and jobs generated by whale watching trips and other commercial ocean tours that include whale watching as a component. The study also characterizes the ocean tour boat industry on an island-by-island basis, and highlights the economic impact of the ocean tour boat industry as a whole. Finally, the report identifies issues of concern that currently confront government and the ocean recreation industry. The study is based on research conducted from February to July of 1999.

RESULTS BY TRIP TYPE

This section presents an analysis of Hawai`i's ocean tour boat industry that is organized by trip type. For example, *0* analyzes the market for whale watching tours. It compares whale watching on the Big Island, Kaua`i, Maui and O`ahu in terms of revenues, number of passengers, prices and other market characteristics. *Results by Island,* on the other hand, organizes the study results by island. It is hoped that by presenting the results in both ways, the study will be more useful to a wide range of potential users.

The results presented in **Results by Trip Type** and **Results by Island** are based on research conducted from February to July 1999. The core of the research consisted of two surveys that were administered in Hawai`i.[6] The first was an "operator survey" that was distributed to ocean tour operators on the Big Island, Kaua`i, Maui and O`ahu. The results of that survey form the basis of the study's direct revenue estimates. In addition, a "passenger survey" was administered to ocean tour passengers on Maui. This survey's results characterized the importance of humpbacks to visitors in the context of the ocean tour boat industry as well as the broader tourism market. The two surveys were supplemented with interviews of key participants, reviews of industry advertising and publications, and other research. A more detailed description of the study methodology is presented in Appendix A.

<u>Whale Watching Tours</u>

Overview

The primary objective of this study was to assess the economic impact of humpback whales on the Hawai`i ocean tour boat industry. As a result, the primary focus of the study was the whale watching tours provided throughout Hawai`i during the 1999 whale watching season. For the purposes of this report, the 1999 whale watching season was defined as December 15, 1998 to April 15, 1999. Although the dates used by some operators varied slightly, a four-month season was fairly constant across operators and islands.

For the purposes of this study, a whale watching trip is defined as an ocean tour that is primarily advertised as a whale watching tour. This definition may sound redundant, but it is stated here to distinguish whale watching trips from other types of trips that feature whale watching as one of several activities or attractions (*e.g.*, snorkeling tours). These latter trips—along with the contribution that humpbacks make to them—are described in subsequent sections.

---

[6] See Appendix B for sample copies of the survey.

Whale watching trips are offered throughout the islands. They are generally two hours long, and this time is spent searching the ocean for humpbacks to approach and view. Most whale watching tours feature on-board naturalists who educate passengers about the natural history of humpbacks, and interpret the behavior of whales encountered during the trip. By federal regulations, vessel operators are prohibited from approaching humpbacks within 100 yards.[7] Even with this 100-yard restriction, however, passengers are often able to get a good view of humpbacks, and the humpbacks occasionally approach vessels within 100 yards. Humpbacks are seen on almost all trips during the whale watching season, and virtually all whale watching operators offer a "guarantee" that enables passengers to return for a free additional trip if whales are not sighted on the first trip. For the privilege of encountering humpbacks at close proximity, thousands of visitors purchase whale watching tour tickets during the 1999 whale season.

Revenues and Other Characteristics

Whale watching tours generated approximately $11 million in direct revenues during the 1999 whale watching season. Fifty-two vessels offered an average of 87 whale watching trips statewide each day in 1999. For the whale season as a whole, these vessels took a total of approximately 370,000 passengers whale watching in Hawai`i in 1999. The total economic impact of commercial whale watching in 1999 was $19 million. This figure includes direct, indirect and induced revenues. Commercial whale watching supported the equivalent of 277 full-time jobs in Hawai`i in 1999. Both of these figures—total economic impact on jobs generated—were calculated by applying multipliers from the 1992 Hawai`i State Input-Output Model to this study's 1999 whale watching direct revenue estimate. Table 2 summarizes the total statewide results, and also highlights key whale watching industry characteristics for the four islands studied.

As Table 2 shows, Maui is the heart of the whale watching industry, accounting for 64 percent of 1999 passengers and 55 percent of 1999 revenues. As this discrepancy between the share of passengers and revenues indicates, prices for Maui whale watches are significantly lower than prices on other islands, averaging $26 per person, $10 lower than the average price on O`ahu, the island with the next-lowest average price. This suggests a higher level of competition in the whale watching market on Maui than on the other islands. This higher level of competition probably results from the fact that Maui has the longest and strongest history of commercial whale watching. The longer time period has enabled more competitors to enter the whale watching business on Maui than on other islands. Interviews with whale watch operators on Maui and the Big Island confirm this explanation, although the evidence is anecdotal.

---

[7] These regulations are found in the Code of Federal Regulations at 50 CFR 222.31.

Table 2: Key Characteristics of Hawai`i's Whale Watching Industry, 1999[8]

	Big Island	Kaua`i	Maui	O`ahu	Totals
Passengers/Day	349	153	1,989	609	3,100
% of All Passengers	11%	5%	64%	20%	100%
Direct Revenues ($Millions)	1.6	0.9	6.1	2.6	11.3
% of Total Revenues	14%	8%	55%	23%	100%
Total Economic Impact ($ Millions)	2.8	1.6	10.5	4.4	19.3
# Vessels	13	7	28	4	52
Total # Trips/Day	14	7	60	6	87
Average Price/Person	$ 39	$ 51	$ 26	$ 36	$ 31

The Role of Humpbacks in the Sale of Other Ocean Tours

The primary objective of this study is to estimate the ocean tour boat revenues that are attributable to the presence of humpbacks in Hawaiian waters. The most obvious component of these revenues is generated by trips that are exclusively whale watching tours. And as the prior section indicates, whale watching tour revenues make a significant contribution to Hawai`i's economy. However, whale watching is a component of several other types of ocean tours during the whale season. For example, snorkel trips often stop to whale watch on the way out to a snorkel site or on the way back in. Many sunset cruises whale watch in addition to providing drinks, pupus and sightseeing opportunities. Given that whale watching is a component of a variety of ocean tours, this study hypothesized that whales play a role in tourists' decisions to buy these "multi-activity" trips. This section attempts to quantify the role that whale watching plays in the sales of these trips by drawing on research conducted on Maui as part of this study.

One indication of the importance of humpbacks in the broader ocean tour boat industry is the presence of whales in the industry's advertising. In many cases, whale watching is prominently advertised as one of several activities that tour passengers are purchasing when they buy tickets for an ocean tour. To determine the importance of humpbacks in ocean tour advertising, a sample of advertisements from rack cards and tourist magazines (*e.g.* Maui Activities) on Maui and the Big Island was examined. The ads were primarily for snorkel trips, but also included dinner cruises, sunset cruises and performance sailing. The cards and magazines were collected at airports on Maui and the Big Island. The sample included every rack card that was available at the airports on the days that the sample was collected. Thus, although the

---

[8] Note that the revenue and economic impact figures presented in this table do not include any snorkeling trip revenues. Some of the totals presented in the Executive Summary do contain snorkeling revenues. Section *0Other Ocean Tours* discusses this topic in detail.

sample was not random in design, it does represent a broad cross-section of the ocean tour boat industry.

Of the 32 multi-activity trip advertisements collected in this sample, 53 percent included pictures of humpbacks as part of the advertisement. In addition, some advertisements that did not include pictures of whales contained text that referred to whale watching. Combining these two categories, 68 percent of the 32 multi-activity trip ads in the sample included either a photograph of a humpback or a mention of whale watching as component of the trip or both. The emphasis on whale watching in these advertisements indicates that most ocean tour operators—at least on Maui and the Big Island—think that humpbacks add value to their trips, even when those trips have snorkeling or some other activity as the primary emphasis.

Although the prominence of humpbacks in advertising for snorkeling and other multi-activity trips suggests that humpbacks are a factor in selling these trips, it does not reveal anything about the purchase decisions made by passengers. The ocean tour passengers themselves have the best information about why they purchased a certain trip. Thus, to unravel these purchase decisions and quantify the importance of humpbacks in sales of multi-activity trips, a survey was administered to Maui snorkeling and dinner cruise passengers during March and April of 1999 (Appendix B contains a copy of the survey).[9]

The survey was administered in person to passengers at the Lahaina and Ma`alaea harbors and at the Kihei boat ramp. Passengers were surveyed while they waited to board their tour vessels. Each group (family, couple, etc.) that agreed to participate in the survey was asked the following question about why they bought their snorkeling trip or dinner cruise:

"When you chose to go on today's boat trip, how important to you was each of the following activities in percentage terms (should total to 100%): touring/sightseeing; lunch/dinner; snorkeling; scuba; fishing; whale watching; other."

It was further explained to passengers that not all of these categories necessarily applied to their trip, and that they were to allocate percentages to only those activities that motivated them to purchase their trip. The average percentages allocated to the activities listed on the survey are summarized in Table 3.

---

[9] In theory, other approaches could be used. For example, one can compare the prices of bundles of goods that differ only in that one bundle includes an extra component. In a perfect market, the price differential between the two bundles would reveal the marginal value of this extra component. While the whale watching component of multi-activity trips is such an "extra component" of a bundle of goods (*i.e.*, a multi-activity trip), the ocean tour market is imperfect to an extent that likely precludes this type of analysis. In particular, seasonal fluctuations in Hawai`i tourism and corresponding fluctuations in ocean tour demand (and supply, in the case of snorkeling tours) make it difficult to isolate the value added by humpbacks using this price differential technique. As a result, a survey of passengers was considered the most reliable method.

Table 3: Average Importance of Ocean Tour Activities to Maui Passengers Surveyed[10]

Activity	Snorkel Trip Passengers	Dinner Cruise Passengers
Whale Watching	19%	8%
Touring/Sightseeing	14%	29%
Snorkeling	52%	0%
Lunch/Dinner	8%	60%
All Other Activities	8%	3%

As might be expected, snorkeling trip passengers rated snorkeling as the most important reason for going on the trip; on average, passengers stated that snorkeling was 52 percent of the reason that they chose to go. Likewise, dinner was the most important trip component to dinner cruise passengers, accounting for 60 percent of the reason that they chose to go on the trip, on average. Touring/sightseeing was also important to dinner cruise passengers. However, they did not indicate that whale watching was an important factor in their decisions to go on the dinner cruises. Snorkeling passengers, on the other hand, stated on average that whale watching accounted for 19 percent of the reason that they chose to go on a snorkeling trip. Table 4 further breaks down this difference in the importance of whale watching to dinner cruise passengers and snorkeling passengers.

Table 4: Importance of Whale Watching to Maui Snorkeling and Dinner Cruise Passengers[11]

Importance of Whale Watching in Percentage Terms	% of Snorkeling Passengers Responding in This Range	Dinner Cruise Passengers Responding in This Range
1-24%	21%	8%
25-49%	16%	8%
50-100%	21%	5%
Total (whale watching % >0)	57%	21%

Table 4 shows that whale watching is an important factor in the Maui snorkeling trip market, but is less important in the dinner cruise market. More than half of the Maui snorkeling trip passengers who were surveyed—57 percent—indicated that whale watching was one of the reasons that they chose to go on a snorkeling trip (*i.e.,* they allocated 1 percent or more to whale

---

[10] Columns may not total 100% due to rounding.

[11] Each of the three rows in Table 4 corresponds to a range of percentages. The two right columns indicate the percentage of passenger responses that fall into those ranges. For example, the first row is labeled "1-24%." Following this row from left to right, it indicates that 21 percent of Maui snorkeling passengers surveyed identified whale watching as representing between 1 and 24 percent of the reason that they chose to go on their snorkeling trip. Continuing across this row, only 8 percent of Maui dinner cruise passengers gave whale watching a percentage value in this range.

watching). By comparison, only 21 percent of Maui dinner passengers who were surveyed chose whale watching from the list of activities on the survey form.

These data confirm what the above analysis of multi-activity trip advertising suggests; that whale watching is an important selling point for some passengers of multi-activity trips. The survey data most strongly indicate that humpbacks are an important reason that some passengers buy snorkeling trips on Maui during the whale season. The data also provide a means to quantify the impact of whales on the snorkeling market. Table 4 shows that for 21 percent of Maui snorkeling trip passengers who were surveyed, whale watching was at least as important as all other trip activities combined, including snorkeling. Put another way, whale watching was 50 percent or more of the reason that 21 percent of snorkeling passengers chose to buy snorkeling trips.

Given the importance that these passengers place on whale watching, it is likely that some or all of them would not have purchased snorkeling trips in the absence of the opportunity to see humpbacks. To the extent that this is the case, the snorkeling revenues generated by these passengers should be included in the total economic impact of humpbacks on the Hawai`i ocean tour boat industry. While the precise extent of this impact cannot be determined from the survey results, this study assumes that none of these 21 percent of snorkeling passengers would purchase snorkeling trips in the absence of humpbacks.[12] Table 5 summarizes how the attribution of this portion of snorkeling revenues to humpbacks changes the estimates of the economic impact of humpbacks on Hawai`i's ocean tour boat industry.

---

[12] This assumption may overestimate the impact on humpbacks on the purchase decisions of the 21 percent of snorkeling passengers who stated that whale watching accounted for 50 percent or more of their reason for buying a snorkeling trip. However, no similar assumption is made about the remaining 36 percent of snorkeling passengers who named whale watching as between 1 and 49 percent of their reason for purchasing a snorkeling trip. Some of these passengers might not have purchased snorkeling trips in the absence of humpbacks; alternatively, they might have been willing to pay less for a snorkeling trip in the absence of humpbacks. In either case, these revenues would be attributable to humpbacks, but are not counted in this study. Thus, the conclusions drawn here about the impact of humpbacks on the snorkeling tour market utilize the survey data in a conservative fashion. Future research could focus more intensively on the relative importance of humpbacks and other components of multi-activity trips.

Table 5: Addition of a Portion of Snorkeling Revenues to the Economic Impact of Humpbacks on Hawai`i's Ocean Tour Boat Industry (All Revenue Figures Are $Millions)[13]

	Add Maui Snorkel Only	Add Snorkel All Islands
Whale Watching Tour Direct Revenues	11.2	11.2
Snorkeling Revenues During Whale Season	13.9	21.8
21% of Whale Season Snorkeling Revenues	2.7	4.6
Combined Direct Revenues Attributable to Whale Watching	13.9	15.8
Combined Total Economic Impact of Whale Watching	23.8	27.0
Combined Jobs Supported by Whale Watching	342	387

The first row of Table 5 presents this study's estimate of 1999 direct revenues from whale watching trips; the second row shows the estimate of snorkeling trip direct revenues during whale season. The first column of figures only includes Maui snorkeling revenues. The second column of figures includes statewide snorkeling revenues for the 1999 whale season (excluding O`ahu). As row three shows, attributing 21 percent of whale season snorkeling revenues to whale watching adds $2.7-4.5 million in revenues to the $11.2 million whale watching tour direct revenues base. This change also increases the economic impact and jobs attributable to humpbacks as compared with the baseline of whale watching tours, as shown in rows 5 and 6 (See Table 2 for baseline).

Both the "Maui Snorkel Only" and "All Snorkel" scenarios are analyzed because it is unclear whether the results of the passenger survey—which was conducted on Maui—are applicable beyond Maui. Maui has the largest whale watching tour industry of any of the Hawaiian islands, and thus may draw visitors that are more interested in humpbacks. If so, then snorkeling passengers on other islands may value the whale watching component of snorkeling trips less highly than their Maui counterparts. In this case, the snorkeling revenues that can be attributed to humpbacks would be closer to the "Maui Snorkel Only" totals. However, it is also possible that snorkeling passengers on other islands have similar attitudes towards humpbacks, in which case the figures would be closer to the "All Snorkel" column. Regardless, the passenger survey data obtained on Maui strongly suggest that humpbacks motivate some visitors to Hawai`i during whale season to purchase snorkeling trips. The above analysis provides a range of estimates of the dollar value of this "humpback effect" on the snorkeling trip market.

---

[13] Columns may not total 100% due to rounding.

Snorkeling Tours

Overview

Snorkeling tours are an important part of Hawai`i's ocean tour boat industry. In fact, the results of this study suggest that snorkeling may be the largest component on a state-wide basis. As discussed in the previous section, snorkeling tours are closely linked with whale watching during the whale season. Unlike whale watching trips, however, snorkeling tours are offered year-round. The following sections provide estimates of the revenues generated by snorkeling tours on the Big Island, Kaua`i and Maui. The revenue estimates are given for two 1999 time frames: the whale season, and the entire calendar year.

Snorkeling Tour Characteristics

Snorkeling tours are less homogeneous than whale watching tours. One trip might differ from the next in any of the following ways:

- *Snorkeling Destination* On a given island, there are a numerous snorkeling destinations offshore. On Maui, for example, the two primary snorkeling destinations are Lana`i and Molokini. However, trips are offered to other snorkeling spots around Maui as well. Similar variety exists off the coast of other Hawaiian islands.

- *Length of Trip* Most trips are four hours long, but six and eight hour trips are offered as well.

- *Emphasis on Snorkeling* The trips that are included here as "snorkeling trips" vary in the amount of emphasis placed on snorkeling versus other activities. Rack cards and other advertisements illustrate this point. For example, humpback whales are prominent in many Maui snorkel trip advertisements. On Kaua`i, however, the Na Pali coast is the most prominent feature in the advertising for many of the trips included here as snorkeling trips. While most of the Na Pali coast trips include snorkeling, some do not.

In spite of these differences, all trips with snorkeling as a primary emphasis are grouped together for the purposes of this report. This approach entails several assumptions that blur the above-mentioned distinctions, but it does not impact the accuracy of the revenue estimates. This is because most of the data used to generate revenue estimates is company and trip-specific. For example, company and trip-specific rack prices were used in all cases. Vessel-specific capacity data were utilized as well. The only average used is the utilization rate (average number of passengers _ vessel capacity). This was applied to vessels that did not respond to the operator survey, and was constant across snorkel trip vessels for a given island.[14]

---

[14] See Appendix A for more detail on the methodology.

Revenues and Other Characteristics

Snorkeling tours on the Big Island, Kaua`i and Maui generated approximately $24 million in direct revenues during the 1999 whale watching season; based on this finding, it is estimated that snorkeling trips on these islands generated approximately $67 million in direct revenues during the full 1999 calendar year.[15]   An average of 95 snorkeling trips was offered statewide each day during the 1999 whale season. The total economic impact of commercial snorkeling in the full 1999 calendar year is estimated to be $114 million. This figure includes direct, indirect and induced revenues. Snorkeling tours also generated over 1,600 jobs in Hawai`i in 1999.  Both of these figures—total economic impact on jobs generated—were calculated by applying multipliers from the 1992 Hawai`i State Input-Output Model to this study's 1999 snorkeling direct revenue estimate. Table 6 summarizes these results, and indicates how the Big Island, Kaua`i and Maui contribute to the snorkeling tour industry.

Table 6: Key Characteristics of Hawai`i's Snorkeling Tour Industry, 1999

	Big Island	Kaua`i	Maui	Totals
Direct Revenues During Whale Season ($Millions)	3.3	5.6	12.9	21.8
Total 1999 Direct Revenues ($Millions)	10.1	17.1	39.5	66.6
% of Total Revenues	15%	26%	59%	100%
Total Economic Impact ($Millions)	17.2	29.3	67.5	114.0
Average Price/Adult	$ 62	$ 95	$ 79	N/A

As Table 6 indicates, Maui has the largest snorkeling tour industry of these three islands, accounting for 59% of their combined revenues. Kaua`i's snorkeling industry is second largest in terms of revenues.  This is partly due to the high prices for snorkeling tours on Kaua`i, which are $16 and $23 per person higher, on average, than on Maui and the Big Island, respectively. Data obtained from O`ahu operators were not sufficient to enable estimates of O`ahu snorkeling revenues, and no estimates from prior studies were available for this specific segment of the O`ahu ocean tour boat industry.  As a result, no O`ahu snorkeling revenue estimates are presented in Table 6. However, several operators run snorkeling trips off O`ahu, and the omission of an estimate from this report should not be taken to suggest that O`ahu snorkeling revenues are zero.

---

[15] Full-year snorkeling revenues were estimated by extrapolating from the data collected during the whale season. This probably resulted in an underestimate of total 1999 snorkeling revenues, because some of the vessels that run whale watches during the whale season replace the whale watches with snorkeling trips during the remainder of the year. Thus, the full-year snorkeling revenue estimates presented here should be considered conservative.

Dinner Cruises

Overview

O`ahu is the heart of the dinner cruise market. There was a low response rate from ocean tour operators on O`ahu to the study's operator survey, however, making it impossible to create new estimates for O`ahu's dinner cruise segment. Rather than simply omit an estimate for this important part of Hawai`i's ocean tour boat industry, it was decided to update the revenue estimate from a prior study (Markrich 1993).[16] Responses from dinner cruise operators on the neighbor islands were sufficient to enable estimation of dinner cruise revenues for the neighbor islands.

Revenues and Other Characteristics

Dinner cruises on the Big Island, Kaua`i and Maui generated $2.4 million in direct revenues during the 1999 whale watching season. For 1999 as a whole, dinner cruises generated $7.2 million in direct revenues on these islands.[17] Based on prior research, it is estimated that O`ahu dinner cruises generated $39.5 million in direct revenues in 1999. Thus, the total direct revenues generated by dinner cruises state-wide in 1999 is estimated to be $46.7 million; total economic impact is estimated to be $79.8 million in direct, indirect and induced revenues. This estimate is based on the application of the 1992 Hawai`i State Input-Output Model to this study's 1999 dinner cruise direct revenue estimate. Table 7 summarizes these results, and indicates how each of the islands contributes to the dinner cruise market.

Table 7: Key Characteristics of Hawai`i's Dinner Cruise Industry, 1999

	Big Island	Kaua`i	Maui	O`ahu	Totals
Direct Revenues During Whale Season ($Millions)	0.7	N/A	1.7	N/A	N/A
Total 1999 Direct Revenues ($Millions)	2.1	N/A	5.1	[39.5]	46.7
% of Total Revenues	4%	N/A	11%	85%	100%
Total Economic Impact ($ Millions)	3.6	N/A	8.7	[67.5]	79.8

---

[16] See Section *0* for further details on the calculations.

[17] Full-year dinner cruise revenues for these three islands were estimated by extrapolating from the data collected during the whale season.

It is important to note that these estimates do not reflect a shift in the dinner cruise market that occurred in April 1999. At that time, a large vessel that had operated dinner cruises on Maui was shifted to Kaua`i. As a result, the estimates presented here underestimate Kaua`i's 1999 dinner cruise revenues (which are thus shown as "N/A" above), and overestimate Maui's 1999 dinner cruise revenues. Nonetheless, the total estimate of dinner cruise revenues across these two islands should not be greatly affected by this change. O`ahu "direct revenues during whale season" are shown as "N/A" because the estimate presented in this report is based on prior research, which did not base its estimates on a survey conducted during the whale season (Markrich 1993).[18] The O`ahu estimates are bracketed to indicate that they are based on prior research. Finally, as noted in 0, a survey of Maui dinner cruise passengers indicated that whale watching does not play a significant role in the sale of dinner cruise tickets. As a result, no dinner cruise revenues were added to estimate of the total impact of humpbacks on the ocean tour boat industry.

Sunset Cruises

Overview

Sunset Cruises are a component of the ocean tour boat industry throughout the islands. Most sunset cruises are two hours in length. Prices depend on the size and type of vessel, as well as the drinks and/or food included. Whales are featured in many of the advertisements for these trips during whale watching season. However, time limitations prevented the inclusion of sunset cruise passengers in this study's passenger survey. As a result, the role that humpbacks play in the sale of sunset cruises is unknown. Thus, none of the estimated sunset cruise revenues were included in the estimate of the total impact of humpbacks on the ocean tour boat industry and Hawai`i economy. As in the dinner cruise market, data collected from O`ahu operators were not sufficient to estimate the size of the sunset cruise market there.

Revenues and Other Characteristics

Sunset cruises generated $2.3 million in direct revenues on the Big Island, Kaua`i and Maui during the 1999 whale watching season. Total direct revenues for all of 1999 were approximately $7.0 million.[19] The total economic impact of sunset cruises in 1999 was $12.1 million in direct, indirect and induced revenues. This figure is based on the application of the 1992 Hawai`i State Input-Output Model to this study's 1999 sunset cruise direct revenue estimate. Table 8 summarizes these results, and indicates how each of the three islands contributes to the sunset cruise market.

---

[18] See Section 0 for further details on the calculations.

[19] Full-year sunset cruise revenues for these three islands were estimated by extrapolating from the data collected during the whale season.

Table 8: Key Characteristics of Hawai`i's Sunset Cruise Industry, 1999

	Big Island	Kaua`i	Maui	Totals
Direct Revenues During Whale Season ($Millions)	0.5	1.2	0.6	2.3
Total 1999 Direct Revenues ($Millions)	1.5	3.7	1.8	7.0
% of Total Revenues	1%	6%	3%	11%
Total Economic Impact	2.5	6.4	3.1	12.1

Data obtained from O`ahu operators were not sufficient to enable estimates of O`ahu sunset cruise revenues, and no estimates from prior studies were available for this specific segment of the O`ahu ocean tour boat industry. As a result, no O`ahu snorkeling revenue estimates are presented in Table 8. However, several operators run sunset cruises off O`ahu, and the omission of an estimate from this report should not be taken to suggest that O`ahu sunset cruise revenues are zero.

RESULTS BY ISLAND

This section presents an analysis of Hawai`i's ocean tour boat industry that is organized by island. For example, *0* analyzes the ocean tour boat industry on the Big Island. The revenues, economic impact, and other industry characteristics are described, as are the relative contributions of whale watching, snorkeling, dinner cruises and sunset cruises. In addition, the major ports and destination are discussed. Similar analyses are presented in subsequent sections for Kaua`i, Maui and O`ahu.

The Big Island

The Big Island ocean tour boat industry is dominated by snorkeling tours, which account for approximately two-thirds of direct revenues.[20] The primary points of departure are the Kailua-Kona Pier, Keauhou Bay, Honokohau Harbor, and the resorts of the Kohala Coast. Whale watching has grown rapidly in the last several years. Prior to that time, there were one or two operators running whale watching trips on the Big Island. Today, that number has grown to 13. Whale watching prices are higher on the Big Island than on Maui, averaging $39 per person versus Maui's $26 per person.

Table 9: Key Characteristics of the Big Island's Ocean Tour Boat Industry, 1999.

Ocean Tour Segment	Direct Revenues ($Millions)	Total Economic Impact ($Millions)	Jobs Supported
Whale Watching	1.6	2.8	40
Snorkeling	10.1	17.2	247
Dinner Cruises	2.1	3.6	52
Sunset Cruises	1.5	2.5	36
Total	15.3	26.1	375

Big Island operators expressed several concerns about their industry. First, they are concerned about the impact of the Navy's Low Frequency Active Sonar testing off the Big Island during the 1998 whale season. Most of the operators interviewed believe that the number of humpbacks in Big Island waters was substantially lower in 1999 than in previous years. They further believe that the LFAS testing is to blame. The Navy recently released its Draft Environmental Impact Statement for deployment of the LFAS system (U.S. Navy 1999). With regard to the Big Island tests, the EIS states that "it was believed that marine mammals exposed to RLs (received levels) near 140 dB would depart the area. However, data from the [the study]

---

[20] As defined in this report, the ocean tour boat industry does not include charter fishing, which is a major commercial ocean recreation activity on the Big Island.

did not support this...breeding humpback whales remained in their area off the 'Big Island' of Hawaii." The EIS models predict that 2.55 percent of humpbacks in the Eastern North Pacific would be potentially affected by deployment of SURTASS LFAS on an annual basis, under the conditions of the preferred alternative. In the fall of 1999, the Navy held hearings on the EIS and accepted written comments.

In addition, Big Island operators expressed concern about the impact of aquarium collecting on reef fish populations. While this concern was addressed by legislation in 1998, operators are disappointed at the slow pace of implementing regulations. Since operators were interviewed in early 1999, however, DLNR has issued proposed regulations, and held public hearings about the proposed regulations on the Big Island.[21] Finally, some operators expressed concerns about growing conflicts between types of ocean operators and users. In particular, kayak operators and traditional tour companies are competing for access to some Big Island ocean areas.

Kaua`i

Kaua`i's ocean tour boat industry is in a state of transition. The largest segment of the industry in the late eighties and early nineties was the Na Pali coast tours that were run out of Hanalei. Opposition to these tours grew along with the industry, leading to a polarized debate about whether and how they should be allowed to continue. In 1998, Governor Cayetano made a decision to close the Hanalei ocean tour boat industry. A handful of operators were allowed to continue operations on a temporary basis; these operators have sued the State and are continuing to operate under a court order.

The Hanalei shutdown has led to dramatic changes in Kaua`i's ocean tour boat industry. Although several Hanalei operators have simply exited the business, most have adapted by moving their operations to Kaua`i's West coast, particularly the Port Allen small boat harbor. This shift has produced a difficult situation for everyone involved. From the perspective of operators, the shift has been somewhat successful, and for this the operators credit the cooperation of Department of Transportation. Nonetheless, problems remain. For example, operators complain that their customers have been denied access to harbor facilities. From the perspective of local residents and existing harbor users, the shift of the industry to Port Allen has produced an undesirable influx of traffic and tourists. The shift to Port Allen has also favored larger vessels because the trip to the Na Pali coast is longer from Port Allen.

Thus, there are a number of issues to be settled before the Kaua`i ocean tour boat industry stabilizes. In spite of the recent changes and current instability, however, the industry continues to generate large revenues on Kaua`i. The Na Pali coast scenery and snorkeling are the main attractions on most Kaua`i ocean tours. In general, these tours are longer and more

---

[21] The proposed regulations are pursuant to Subtitle 5, Chapter 188F of Hawai`i's Revised Statutes.

expensive than similar trips offered on Maui and the Big Island. Whale watching tours are also popular on Kaua`i, and operators reported a higher than average number of whales during the 1999 whale watching season. Table 10 summarizes key characteristics of Kaua`i's ocean tour boat industry.

Table 10: Key Characteristics of Kaua`i's Ocean Tour Boat Industry, 1999

Ocean Tour Segment	Direct Revenues ($Millions)	Total Economic Impact ($Millions)	Jobs Supported
Whale Watching	0.9	1.6	23
Snorkeling	17.1	29.3	420
Dinner Cruises	N/A	N/A	N/A
Sunset Cruises	3.7	6.4	92
Total	21.8	37.3	535

It should be noted that the figures in Table 10 do not reflect a shift in the dinner cruise market that occurred in April 1999. At that time, a large vessel that had operated dinner cruises on Maui was shifted to Kaua`i. As a result, the estimates presented here underestimate Kaua`i's 1999 dinner cruise revenues (which are thus shown as "N/A" above), and overestimate Maui's 1999 dinner cruise revenues. Nonetheless, the total estimate of dinner cruise revenues across these two islands should not be greatly affected by this change.

Maui

Maui leads two of the ocean tour boat industry segments discussed in this report, whale watching and snorkeling. Maui's whale watching industry generated $6.1 million in direct revenues during the 1999 whale season, approximately half of the state total. Maui operators ran 60 whale watches per day during that time, taking approximately 2,000 passengers whale watching each day.

Maui snorkeling tours generated nearly $40 million in direct revenue during the full 1999 calendar year. Although O`ahu snorkeling tour estimates could not be made, it is unlikely that O`ahu's snorkeling revenues would approach those of Maui. During the 1999 whale season, Maui operators ran 48 snorkeling trips per day, carrying over 1,650 total snorkelers per day.

The small boat harbors at Lahaina and Ma`alaea are the major points of departure for Maui's ocean tours. Ocean tours also depart from the Kihei boat ramp, the Mala Wharf and Ka`anapali beach. There are numerous snorkeling destinations around Maui. Molokini crater is by far the most popular, hosting an estimated 850 snorkelers per day. Most Molokini trips depart from Ma`alaea harbor in the morning. They generally include lunch and a second snorkeling stop before returning around noon. Most snorkel tours run out of Ma`alaea are morning tours, stopping at Molokini and a second snorkeling spot. Molokini was the top snorkeling spot during the 1999 whale season, hosting approximately 850 snorkelers per day. Lahaina snorkeling tours are fewer and more varied in destination than the Ma`alaea tours. Lana`i was a popular destination, hosting approximately 270 snorkelers per day. Table 11 summarizes the economic impacts of Maui's ocean tour boat industry.

Table 11: Key Characteristics of Maui's Ocean Tour Boat Industry, 1999

Ocean Tour Segment	Direct Revenues ($Millions)	Total Economic Impact ($Millions)	Jobs Supported
Whale Watching	6.1	10.5	151
Snorkeling	39.5	67.5	969
Dinner Cruises	5.1	8.7	125
Sunset Cruises	1.8	3.1	45
Total	52.5	89.8	1,290

It should be noted that the figures in Table 11 do not reflect a significant change that occurred in Maui's ocean tour boat industry during April, 1999. At that time, a large vessel that had previously been used on Maui was moved to the Kaua`i market. Because most survey data was collected prior to this move, estimation of the change in Maui revenues was not possible in this study. The major impact of this omission is that the dinner cruises revenue estimate for Kaua`i is understated, and the Maui dinner cruise revenue estimate is overstated. However, the estimate of total dinner cruise revenues across these two islands should be largely unaffected by this change.

Several Maui operators expressed concerns about their industry. While operators are not satisfied with harbor facilities, many seem resigned to the present conditions, particularly in light of the controversy surrounding plans to modify Ma`alaea harbor. A more achievable goal voiced by several operators is an increased government role in funding and expediting the permit process for installation of new mooring pins and maintenance of existing pins. These operators think that additional pins would prevent reef damage from occurring at heavily-used snorkeling sites throughout Maui waters. However, they see government resource agencies as obstructing rather than facilitating progress in this area.

O`ahu

Several large companies account for the majority of O`ahu's ocean tour revenues. These companies operate large vessels, which range in passenger capacity from 250-1500. During the whale watching season, these large vessels are used primarily for whale watching, coastal cruises and dinner cruises. The large vessels operate out of Honolulu harbor and Kewalo Basin. In addition to the large companies and vessels, there are a number of small vessels in O`ahu's ocean recreation industry. Catamarans operate off of Waikiki, taking visitors on short ocean tours. In addition, small vessels operate from Kane`ohe Bay and Haleiwa.

As discussed in prior sections, O`ahu's large ocean tour operators did not respond to this study's operator survey. As a result, it was impossible to generate direct revenue estimates for O`ahu's snorkeling, dinner cruise and sunset cruise markets. A whale watching estimate was developed based on interviews with key participants and direct observation of several O`ahu whale watches during the 1999 whale season. Based on this information, it is estimated that O`ahu whale watching tours generated $2.6 million in direct revenues during the 1999 whale season. The total economic impact of these tours was $4.4 million in direct, indirect and induced revenues.

Prior studies have demonstrated that the O`ahu dinner cruise market is a large component of Hawai`i's ocean tour boat industry. As noted above, however, data limitations made it impossible to generate revenue estimates for this important industry segment. As a result, a prior estimate of dinner cruise revenues was updated and included in this study's direct revenue totals to present a more accurate view of Hawai`i's ocean tour boat industry as a whole. More specifically, the 1990 dinner cruise revenue estimate from the Markrich study (1993) was adjusted for inflation and then used as a 1999 direct revenue estimate for the O`ahu dinner cruise market.[22] Based on this calculation, it is estimated that the O`ahu dinner cruises generated $39.5 million in direct revenues in 1999. The total economic impact of these cruises was $67.5 million in direct, indirect and induced revenues; the industry also supported 969 jobs. Table 12 summarizes the economic impacts of O`ahu's ocean tour boat industry.

Table 12: Key Characteristics of O`ahu's Ocean Tour Boat Industry, 1999

Ocean Tour Segment	Direct Revenues ($Millions)	Total Economic Impact ($Millions)	Jobs Supported
Whale Watching	2.6	4.4	63
Snorkeling	N/A	N/A	N/A
Dinner Cruises	[39.5]	[67.5]	[969]
Sunset Cruises	N/A	N/A	N/A
Total	42.0	71.9	1,032

Note that the dinner cruise figures are bracketed to indicate that they are adapted from a prior study. While relying on a prior study is somewhat problematic, omitting O`ahu's dinner cruise industry from this study was thought to be more problematic, in that it would greatly

---

[22] See Section *0* for further details on the calculations.

understate the economic impact of Hawai`i's ocean tour boat industry. In addition, the assumptions underlying the inclusion of the dinner cruise revenue estimate are conservative. No growth in O`ahu dinner cruise revenues is assumed to have occurred between 1990-1999, despite findings of industry growth on the neighbor islands. In addition, it should be noted that no snorkeling or sunset cruise revenue estimates were included. The data collected for this study did not enable generation of estimates, and prior studies did not isolate these market segments, making it impossible to adapt prior estimates as was done for the dinner cruise market.

CONCLUSIONS

Humpback whales have a large impact on Hawai`i's ocean tour boat industry and economy. During the 1999 whale season, ocean tour boat direct revenues attributable to humpbacks were estimated to range from $11-16 million. The total economic impact of humpbacks during the 1999 whale season was $19-27 million in direct, indirect and induced revenues. These revenues generated an estimated 280-390 jobs in Hawai`i.

The broader ocean tour boat industry has an even larger impact on Hawai`i's economy. The four ocean tour boat industry segments targeted for this report—whale watches, snorkeling tours, sunset cruises and dinner cruises—generated an estimated $132 million in direct revenues in 1999. These revenues supported more than 3,200 jobs, and the total economic impact of the industry was $225 million in direct, indirect and induced revenues.

The scope of this study is not identical to the scope of prior studies, making it difficult to track the industry across time. In particular, no prior studies have estimated the revenues of whale watching as a distinct ocean tour industry segment. However, a prior study of Hawai`i's ocean recreation industry—which is the basis for this study's O`ahu dinner cruise revenue estimates—had a similar overall scope, in that it covered "tour boats," and included many of the same types of tours covered in this study. This prior study, which estimated 1990 revenues, included several industry segments (*e.g.*, submarine tours) that were not included in the present study. As a result, comparison of the present results with the prior study would tend to understate growth that has occurred since 1990. Nonetheless, the total revenue estimates from the prior study do provide a basis for a rough assessment of growth in the industry during the 1990s. Table 13 shows how revenues have changed on the Big Island, Kaua`i, and Maui during that time period.

In inflation-adjusted terms, the industry has grown in the 1990s, against the backdrop of a relatively stagnant tourist economy. The Big Island has shown the largest growth, and is almost 50 percent larger than in 1990. The Kaua`i and Maui ocean tour industries have grown more slowly. O`ahu changes are omitted because a new total estimate for O`ahu could not be generated with the study's data.

Table 13: Changes in Total Ocean Tour Boat Direct Revenues, 1990-1999[23]

	Big Island	Kaua`i	Maui	O`ahu
1990 Revenues ($ millions of 1990 dollars)	7.2	12.25	29.9	N/A
1990 Revenues ($ millions of 1999 dollars)	9.0	15.3	37.4	N/A
1999 Revenues	13.1	18.7	45.2	N/A
% Change	45%	22%	21%	N/A
Compound Annual Growth Rate	4.3%	2.2%	2.1%	N/A

Because whale watching was not isolated in the 1990 study, it is impossible to track the growth of this industry segment, which is most strongly dependent on humpbacks. However, the estimates contained in this report provide a reference point for future studies. In addition to revisiting the economic impact of humpbacks on the ocean tour boat industry, future studies could measure the impact of humpbacks on other parts of Hawai`i's economy.

---

[23] Unadjusted 1990 figures are from Markrich 1993. The inflation adjustment factor was derived from U.S. Bureau of Labor, Honolulu Consumer Price Index figures for 1990 and 1999. Also, note that the 1999 revenue totals do not match the totals shown in Table 1 and elsewhere because they are the operators' revenues rather than total revenues. The Markrich study presented operator revenues, without commissions paid to middlemen. Thus, to enable a comparison of the present results to the Markrich study, commissions were subtracted out to obtain the total 1999 operator revenues. See
Table 19 and supporting text for further information.

REFERENCES

Hawai`i Department of Business, Economic Development and Tourism. 1998. *The Hawai`i Input-Output Study, 1992 Benchmark Report.*

Markrich, M. 1993. *Status Report (1990) of the Economic Characteristics of Ocean Recreation in Hawai`i.* Ocean Resources Branch, Hawai`i Department of Business, Economic Development and Tourism.

U.S. Navy. 1999. *Draft Overseas Environmental Impact Statement and Environmental Impact Statement for Surveillance Towed Array Sensor System Low Frequency Active (SURTASS LFA) Sonar.*

APPENDIX A: METHODOLOGY

Overview of Methodology

This section presents a description of the study's methodology. It is organized by the three phases of the study, each of which is described below: study design; data collection; and data analysis.

Study Design

The primary objective of the study was to estimate the economic impact of humpback whales on Hawai`i's ocean tour boat industry. Economic impact measures the impact of an industry or project in terms of revenues generated (direct, indirect and induced) and jobs supported. It is sometimes confused with economic net benefit, a different economic measure. Economic net benefit measures the difference between costs and benefits. For consumers, this is the difference between price and willingness to pay; for producers, it is the difference between production cost and price. Economic benefit is an important measure, and has been studied in relation to wildlife and recreation in other places. However, measurement of economic benefits requires detailed information about producers' costs and consumers' willingness to pay. Collection of this information was not feasible in the project time frame. By comparison, economic impact is more easily estimated, and is also a useful measure, as it provides a way to gauge the relative size of industries within a defined geographic area. More specifically, the research focused on creating *direct* revenue estimates, which could then be used in conjunction with existing multipliers to estimate jobs supported as well as indirect and induced revenues. Direct revenues in this case are the monies paid by passengers who purchase ocean tours. Thus, the main design task was to devise a method for estimating ocean tour boat industry direct revenues and a means for determining the role of humpbacks in creating those revenues.

This study partly replicated the approach of prior studies, in that the primary data source for the direct revenue estimates was a voluntary survey distributed to ocean tour operators. The operator survey (shown in *0*) asked for information about marketing channels used, prices charged per trip, types and numbers of trips offered, number of passengers per trip, and vessel capacities. This data enabled the calculation of vessel-specific estimates of direct revenues; the data also provided information about utilization rates (i.e., average number of passengers per trip ÷ vessel capacity), which were used to estimate the revenues of vessels that did not respond to the voluntary survey. The operator survey was supplemented with a survey of ocean tour passengers (shown in *0*). This passenger survey was designed to determine the role that humpbacks play in the markets for ocean tours that include whale watching as one of several components. *0* explains in detail how the operator and passenger survey data were used to create direct revenue estimates.

The target universe of ocean tour operators was defined in conjunction with the process of drafting the survey documents. The guiding principle was to include any operator of an ocean tour that included whale watching as a component. By applying this principle to the array of ocean tours offered in Hawai`i during the whale season, it was decided to target operators of whale watches, snorkeling tours, sunset cruises and dinner cruises. This definition excluded some segments of Hawai`i's ocean tour boat industry, but was thought to include all types of trips that have even a small whale watching component.

Throughout the design process, ocean tour operators and government representatives were asked to evaluate the approach and draft materials. This input both confirmed the general study approach and yielded numerous suggestions for improving the survey materials. The last step in the design process was to test the operator survey with several operators prior to distributing it statewide.

Data Collection

The first data collection step was to assemble a database that contained information about all ocean tour operators in the target universe (*i.e.*, those that operate whale watches, snorkeling trips, sunset cruises or dinner cruises). Information was drawn from a variety of sources, including marketing material, ocean tour boat industry studies, and telephone inquiries. Contact information, vessel capacities, trip schedules, and prices were obtained from these sources for all operators in the target universe. The database included approximately one hundred Hawai`i ocean tour companies, who collectively operate more than 150 vessels.

Utilizing the operator contact information, the operator survey was then mailed to all target ocean tour operators in Hawai`i. A cover letter of support for the project, signed by industry and government representatives, was included with the survey, along with a fact sheet explaining the study's goals and methodology. Follow-up phone calls were used to answer questions about the project and to encourage operators to complete and return the survey. Several operators expressed concerns about the survey, most often with regard to confidentiality or the potential use of the study's results to target the industry for increased taxation. For the most part, however, operators were interested in the project and willing to participate by completing the survey. Although no large O`ahu operators participated in the survey, response rates were high on the Big Island, Kaua`i and Maui, as shown in Table 14.

The first row of Table 14 shows the number of companies that were in the target universe on the Big Island, Kaua`i and Maui; the second row indicates the number of companies from the target universe that completed the operator survey. Finally, the third row indicates the capacity-weighted response rates for each island.[24] Capacity-weighted response rates were used to give a more accurate picture of the portion of the industry that participated in the study. As the table

---

[24] The capacity-weighted response rate for each island is calculated as: (sum of vessel capacities of all operators that completed the survey) _ (the total vessel capacity of all operators in the target universe).

shows, operator survey response rates were strong for these three islands, particularly on Maui and the Big Island.

Table 14: Capacity-Weighted Response Rates for the Big Island, Kaua`i and Maui

	Big Island	Kaua`i	Maui
Target Universe (# Companies)	16	21	68
# of Responses	13	9	28
Capacity-Weighted Response Rate	57%	40%	55%

The completed surveys yielded important information the quantity and prices of tours offered, the average numbers of passengers, tour prices, and marketing methods. Related data was collected from other sources as well. Rack cards, tourist magazines and telephone inquiries, for example, were used to determine the tour schedules and prices of operators that did not complete the operator survey. In addition, spot observations were used to check the accuracy of the passenger numbers provided on completed survey. Finally, interviews with representatives of the ocean tour boat industry were conducted to collect information about the context in which the ocean tour boat industry operates.

As noted above, information about ocean tour passengers was collected by means of a survey that was administered to them as they waited to board snorkeling and dinner cruise vessels. These surveys provided data about two important issues: 1) the relative importance of a set of activities (including whale watching) in passengers' decisions to purchase a snorkel or dinner cruise; 2) and the extent to which the presence of humpbacks in Hawai`i was a factor in ocean tour passengers' choice of Hawai`i as a vacation destination.

Data Analysis

By combining data from all of the above sources, it was possible to estimate ocean tour boat industry revenues for the 1999 whale watching season. By extrapolating from these estimates, ocean tour boat industry revenues were estimated for the entire 1999 calendar year. These estimates are presented throughout the preceding sections of this document. The process that was used to develop the majority of these estimates is described in step-by-step fashion in this section. This process was used to develop all of the ocean tour revenue estimates presented in this study for the islands of Hawai`i, Kaua`i and Maui. O`ahu ocean tour boat industry revenue estimates could not be developed using the process described below because of low survey response rates from O`ahu operators. However, O`ahu whale watching revenues were estimated using data collected from several non-survey sources, including observations of trips

39

and interviews with key industry representatives. Similar estimates based on non-survey data sources were not possible for O`ahu's other ocean tour boat industry segments. With these caveats in mind, the following paragraphs describe the steps by which study data were analyzed to produce the ocean tour boat industry revenue estimates presented in this report.

1. *For companies that completed the operator survey, revenues were estimated directly from the survey data provided.* As noted above, the survey requested information about the types of trips offered, the number of each type of trip offered per week, the price per person, and the average number of passengers per trip. By combining these data, it was possible to calculate estimates of revenues per week for each trip type.[25]

2. *Data from the operator surveys were used to calculate the weighted-average utilization rates for each island and trip type.* The results are shown in Table 15.

Table 15: *Weighted Average Utilization Rates by Trip Type and Island*

Trip Type	Big Island	Kaua`i	Maui
Whale Watch	66%	50%	57%
Snorkel Trip	65%	74%	70%
Dinner Cruise	50%	N/A	50%
Sunset Cruise	47%	75%	52%

Each utilization rate represents the average percentage of vessel capacity used for that island-trip combination. In other words, it is the average number of passengers per trip as a percentage of vessel capacity. For example, the survey data collected from Big Island operators indicated that whale watching trips were running at 66 percent of vessel capacity; *i.e.,* 1999 whale watching trips ran two-thirds full on the Big Island in 1999, according to surveys submitted from there.

These utilization rates were calculated on a capacity-weighted basis. This means that for each island/trip-type combination, the utilization rate was calculated as:

(sum of reported passengers per trip for that island/trip-type combination) _ (sum of maximum vessel capacity of these operators).

For example, nine Big Island whale watching operators completed the operator survey. The sum of the number of passengers per whale watching trip reported by these companies was 263. In addition, the sum of the vessel capacities reported by these

---

[25] The four types of trips for which revenues estimates were made were whale watching, snorkeling, dinner cruise and sunset cruise.

companies was 400. Thus, the Big Island whale watching utilization rate was calculated to be 66 percent (263 _ 400). Similar calculations were made for the other island/trip-type combinations shown in Table 15. These utilization rates were one of the keys to estimating the revenues of operators who did not respond to the survey, as discussed in the next step.

3. *The revenues of vessels that did not respond to the survey were estimated by combining publicly available price, trip schedule and capacity data with a utilization rate estimate based on survey data.* Rack cards, tourist magazines (*e.g.*, This Week), and phone inquiries were used to develop profiles for operators within the target universe who did not complete a survey. Each operator's profile included data about vessel capacities, type and number of trips offered per week, and price per passenger. For each operator, the appropriate utilization rate was then used to estimate the number of passengers per trip for all trips offered by that operator.

    For example, take the hypothetical case of a Maui whale watching operator who did not respond to the survey. Based on marketing information and phone inquiries to the operator, it was determined that this operator offered one whale watching trip per day during the 1999 whale season. The advertised rack price of the whale watch was $25, and the maximum capacity of the operator's vessel was 49 passengers. Based on the analysis of data submitted by other Maui whale watching operators, it was determined that the weighted average utilization rate for whale watching trips on Maui was 57 percent during the 1999 whale watching season (see step 2, above). Using all of this information, the estimated gross revenues per whale watching trip for the hypothetical Maui operator was calculated as follows:

    Gross Revenues Per Whale Watching Trip = Rack Price _ Passenger Capacity _ Weighted Average Utilization

    Gross Revenues Per Whale Watching Trip = $25 per passenger _ 49 passenger per trip capacity _ 57 percent weighted-average utilization for Maui whale watching trips

    Gross Revenues Per Whale Watching Trip = $698 per whale watching trip

    Similar calculations were made for all vessels whose operators did not submit a survey. For all of the estimates, price, capacity and schedule data specific to each operator were combined with utilization rates specific to the island and trip type. Revenues per week were then estimated based on the trip schedule data that had been collected.

4. *Total gross ocean tour boat industry revenues for the 1999 whale season and full 1999 calendar year were calculated.* After completion of the above three steps, estimates of revenues per week had been developed for every operator in the target universe. These estimates were specific to the four trip types that were included within the scope of the study. For each island, estimated revenues per week were summed by trip type. To

41

generate revenue estimates for the 1999 whale season, these totals were multiplied by 17, which is the number of weeks in the December 15, 1998 to April 15, 1999 period used to define the 1999 whale season. This resulted in total revenue estimates by island and trip type for the 1999 whale season. Revenue estimates for the full 1999 calendar year were developed in a similar fashion; the estimates of total revenues per week for each island were multiplied by 56 weeks per year.

It is important to note that the aggregate estimates presented in this report are a mixture of 1999 whale season revenue estimates and full 1999 calendar year estimates. Whale watching revenue estimates presented in the report correspond to the 1999 whale season, for obvious reasons. However, the revenue estimates for snorkeling tours, dinner cruises, and sunset cruises are for the full 1999 calendar year. The only exception to this statement is in *0*, which discusses the relationship between snorkeling tours and whales during the whale season.

It is likely that extrapolating from data collected during the 1999 whale season to the full 1999 calendar year resulted in understating 1999 full-year revenues. The reason is that during the remainder of the year, operators offer other ocean tours in the slots occupied by whale watching tours during the whale seasons. Determining precisely how the tour mix changed after the whale season was beyond the scope of this study. In spite of this limitation of the data collected for this study, it was decided that estimates of full year revenues for snorkeling tours, dinner cruises and sunset cruises would be more useful than if revenue estimates for these trip types were limited to the 1999 whale season.

Similarly, it was decided that updating prior estimates of O`ahu's dinner cruise revenues would be more useful than simply omitting the estimate. This industry segment was considered to be too important to leave out of the study. However, data limitations made it impossible to create new revenue estimates. The O`ahu market is dominated by a handful of large companies, and data were lacking for all of them. Exacerbating the lack of data was the fact that analysis of the O`ahu dinner cruise market is more complex than analysis of the other ocean tour boat industry segments included in this report. First, several of the vessels that serve O`ahu's dinner cruise market are very large, providing a wide range in possible utilization rates. These vessels also offer a variety of price points on each trip, depending on the food and amenities that a passenger wants to purchase. Thus, given the complex O`ahu dinner cruise market and a lack of operator-provided data, it was impossible to create new estimates of the O`ahu dinner cruise market. Nonetheless, this market segment is such a large part of the ocean tour boat industry that it would have been confusing, and possibly misleading, to present aggregate economic impact estimates for Hawai`i's ocean tour boat industry without including it. Thus, it was decided to update the Markrich estimate for inflation using the CPI-derived adjustment factor described in Appendix A.

5. *The portion of non-whale watching tour revenues attributable to humpbacks was calculated.* This calculation utilized the 1999 whale season revenue estimates, along with data collected in the passenger survey. The methodology used for this set of estimates is described in detail in *0*, and is not repeated here. However, the information presented there is supplemented here by information about the scope of the operator survey, which is shown in Table 14.

Table 16: Characteristics of the Passenger Survey Sample Universe

Number of passenger groups surveyed	108
Total number of passengers in groups surveyed	349
Number of snorkel operators represented	5
Number of dinner cruises represented	2

As the table indicates, 108 groups of snorkeling and dinner cruise passengers were surveyed on Maui. The total number of passengers in these groups was 349 (*i.e.*, there were approximately 3 passengers in each group surveyed). The passengers included in the survey were customers of 5 snorkel tour operators and 2 dinner cruise operators.

6. *The effects of differing prices and marketing channels on total revenues was estimated; in addition, the split of total revenues between tour operators and middlemen was estimated.* Hawai`i ocean tour operators use a variety of marketing channels to sell their tours. The prices charged for the same tour may vary by channel. Operators typically advertise a rack price, and will charge the full rack price for trips booked directly. Others will offer discounts for direct bookings. All operators must offer substantial discounts to the middlemen (*e.g.*, activity desks) who sell all of the tours not purchased directly from the operators. The most important middlemen are activity desks. Activity desks purchase tours at a discounted price from operators. The desks are then able to mark up the tickets from this price, and still offer them at a discount from the rack price. The value that the activity desks provide to operators in exchange for their commissions is the ability to sell a high volume of tours. The desks are generally located in high traffic areas such as hotels and shopping areas. They offer a wide range of tours and other services to tourists, making it convenient for tourists to book several activities in one place. Some activity desks also use ocean tour vouchers and discounts as incentives to entice tourists to attend sales seminars on time-shares and rental properties. In general, the activity desk business is dominated by a handful of large firms that serve the mainstream markets; these large firms are complimented by smaller firms that serve specific niches (*e.g.*, travel agents who handle group tours). By and large, activity desks are the most important marketing channel for the ocean tour segments described in this study.

As noted above, the price data that was collected for this study's revenue estimates were full or rack prices. Due to the variance of prices by marketing channels discussed in the prior paragraph, however, revenue estimates based solely on rack prices would result in an overestimate of revenues. Thus, the revenue estimates from the prior steps had to be adjusted to account for the variance in prices in different marketing channels. To obtain data that would enable such an adjustment, the operator surveys asked respondents to identify the percentage of tours sold through: 1) activity desks; 2) directly to passengers; 3) through other channels. Using the responses to this question, capacity-weighted averages were developed for each island, as shown in Table 17.

Table 17: Weighted Averages of the Percentage of Tickets Sold Through Intermediaries, by Island

	Overall Average	Big Island	Kaua`i	Maui
Weighted Average % tickets sold directly	32%	47%	29%	27%
Weighted Average % tickets sold through activity desk or other intermediary	68%	53%	71%	73%
Average Commissions	35%			
Average discount on direct-sold tickets	10%			

As shown in Table 17, the overall capacity-weighted average percentage of tours sold through activity desks or other intermediaries was 68 percent. This varied somewhat by island, with Big Island operators reporting a larger percentage of direct sales than their Kaua`i and Maui counterparts. Regardless of this variation, the data presented in the first two rows of Table 17 clearly indicate the large role played by middlemen in selling ocean tours in Hawai`i. Activity desks accounted for 63 percent of tours sold, or 93 percent of tours sold through intermediaries.

Independent of the survey, additional information was collected about how activity desks impact prices, and how they split revenues with the operators. Row three shows that the average commission charged by activity desks was 35 percent. Commissions, as used in this context, are the percentage discount from rack price that operators give to activity desks and other intermediary sellers. The 35 percent figure used in this study, and shown in Table 17, is based on interviews with ocean tour operators and activity desk representatives. This figure is a point estimate, but commissions vary greatly from operator to operator. Operators with high demand for their tours pay less than this 35 percent average, while operators who struggle to fill their boats may pay as much as 50 percent in commissions to activity desks. However, 35 percent represented the midpoint of the commission ranges provided by operators and activity desk representatives, and is believed to be a good proxy for the average commission.

Row four shows the average discount from rack price offered by activity desks to passengers. Like the estimate of average commissions, this 10 percent figure is a point estimate; it based on information data from activity desk advertising, as well as interviews with operators and activity desk representatives.

By combining all of the data from Table 17, it was possible to adjust direct revenue estimates and quantify how they are split between operators and intermediaries. For example, the weighted-average percentage of ocean tours sold through activity desks and other intermediaries—as reported on the operator surveys—was 73 percent on Maui (see Row 2 of Table 17). The average discount to passengers was 10 percent, and the average commissions were 35 percent. Thus, each dollar of Maui ocean tour revenue, as calculated from the preceding steps, was adjusted my multiplying by the following factor: $(1 - (73 \text{ percent} \times 10 \text{ percent}))$. In other words, on Maui, the effect of discounting in the indirect ocean tour sales channels was a 7.3 percent reduction of direct ocean tour revenues from the rack price-based revenue estimates as calculated in the prior five steps. Similar calculations were made for all tour type/island combinations. The resulting adjusted figures are the direct revenue estimates shown in the "Direct Revenues" columns of Table 1, and elsewhere throughout the report. These estimates include revenues to tour operators *and* intermediary sellers. They were grouped in this study because both types of revenues are attributable to the ocean tour boat industry, and both are expenditures within Hawai`i. Thus, from an economic impact standpoint, revenues to activity desks should be grouped with those of operators to account for the full impact of the industry.

However, it is also useful to look at how revenues are divided between operators and the activity desks. The information contained in Table 17 also enables the estimation of how ocean tour revenues are split between operators and middlemen.[26] The results are shown in Table 18.

---

[26] The formula used to calculate the Desks' share of adjusted revenues is: [% Sold Through Desks _ (% Commission - % Discount)] _ [(1 - % Sold Through Desks) + (% Sold Through Desks _ (1 - % Discount)]

Table 18: Direct Revenue Shares of Operators and Activity Desks

	Overall Average	Big Island	Kaua`i	Maui
% of Revenues to Activity Desks and Other Intermediaries	18%	14%	19%	20%
% of Revenues to Operators	82%	86%	81%	80%

As Table 18 indicates, activity desks and other intermediaries' share of direct revenues was approximately 20 percent. To calculate the shares in dollar terms, the percentages from Table 17 were applied to the direct revenue estimates shown in Table 1. The results are shown in

Table 19.

Jobs supported, as well as induced and indirect revenues, could also be split between operators and intermediaries in a similar fashion. These are discussed in more detail in the next step.

Table 19: Direct Revenues of Operators and Activity Desks in Dollars

Island	Tour Type	Direct Revenues	
		Desks	Operators
Big Island	Whale Watching	0.2	1.4
	Snorkeling	1.4	8.6
	Dinner Cruises	0.3	1.8
	Sunset Cruises	0.2	1.3
	Total	2.1	13.1
Kaua`i	Whale Watching	0.1	0.8
	Snorkeling	2.4	14.7
	Dinner Cruises	N/A	N/A
	Sunset Cruises	0.5	3.2
	Total	3.1	18.7
Maui	Whale Watching	0.9	5.3
	Snorkeling	5.5	33.9
	Dinner Cruises	0.7	4.4
	Sunset Cruises	0.3	1.6
	Total	7.4	45.2
O`ahu	Whale Watching	0.4	2.2
	Snorkeling	N/A	N/A
	Dinner Cruises	N/A	N/A
	Sunset Cruises	N/A	N/A
	Total	0.4	2.2
State-Wide	Whale Watching	1.6	9.7
	Snorkeling	9.4	57.3
	Dinner Cruises	1.0	6.2
	Sunset Cruises	1.0	6.1
	Total	12.9	79.2

7. *The total economic impact of the ocean tour boat industry, including indirect and induced revenues and jobs supported, was calculated by applying the 1992 Hawai`i State Input-Output Model to the study's estimates of direct revenues.* The prior six steps generated the study's 1999 direct revenue estimates for the targeted Hawai`i ocean tour segments. These direct revenue estimates were the objective of the study's primary research—the survey work, interviews, and data collection. Direct revenues are an important measure

of economic impact, but do not tell the whole story. The impact of these dollars spent on ocean tours does not end with the operators and intermediaries. In order to run their businesses, operators need to purchase supplies such as fuel, food, and snorkeling equipment. The portion of these expenditures that remains in Hawai`i is added into the total economic impact of the ocean tour boat industry, and is referred to as indirect revenues. Similarly, employees of operators and intermediaries spend a portion of their wages within Hawai`i; this portion is added into the total economic impact, and is referred to as induced revenues. Finally, all of these revenues—direct, indirect and induced—support jobs.

To calculate the indirect and induced revenues and jobs supported by the ocean tour boat industry, an existing study was used. *The Hawai`i Input-Output Study, 1992 Benchmark Report*, completed in 1998, is a study of how the sectors of Hawai`i's economy interact with each other and with the rest of the world. The information contained in the study includes multipliers, which, when used in conjunction with direct revenue estimates, enable the calculation of indirect and induced revenues and jobs supported. The study does not contain multipliers that are specific to the ocean tour boat industry. As a result, generic multipliers for the tourism industry were utilized. They were obtained from the Hawai`i Department of Business, Economic Development and Tourism.[27] The next step was to apply existing multipliers to the study's direct revenue estimates.

Table 20: Multipliers Used to Determine Total Economic Impact and Jobs Supported

Multiplier Type	Value
Total Economic Impact	1.71
Jobs Supported (# jobs/$ million in direct revenues)	24.55

The first multiplier shown in Table 20 is the total economic impact multiplier. For Hawai`i's tourism industry, its value is 1.71. This means that for each dollar of direct revenues in Hawai`i's tourism industry, there are $0.71 dollars of indirect and induced revenues. Thus, multiplying the study's direct revenue estimates by 1.71 produced the "total economic impact" estimates shown in Table 1 and elsewhere in the report. The second multiplier, "jobs supported," indicates the number of jobs supported by one million dollars in direct revenues. In the case of Hawai`i's tourism industry, this multiplier is 24.55; applying this factor to the study's direct revenue estimates produced the "jobs supported" estimates shown in Table 1 and elsewhere in the report.

---

[27] Xijun Tian, personal communication, July 22, 1999.

APPENDIX B: SAMPLE SURVEYS

<u>Passenger Survey</u>

The following survey was used to collect information from Maui snorkeling tour and dinner cruise passengers about two topics: 1) the reasons that they purchased their ocean tours, and; 2) the importance of humpbacks as a factor in their decision to come to Hawai`i for vacation. The survey was administered to passengers while they were waiting to board their tours at Lahaina and Ma`alaea harbors and the Kihei boat ramp. The survey was designed with assistance from representatives of both the ocean tour boat industry and Hawai`i state government. Further details about the results of the survey were presented earlier in this paper.

Ocean Recreation Survey

The National Oceanic and Atmospheric Administration are conducting a survey to estimate the economic benefits associated with ocean recreation in Hawai`i. The survey data will be used to develop a report on Hawai`i's ocean recreation industry. By taking a few minutes to answer this questionnaire, you can provide the data needed to complete this important effort. Thank you for your assistance!

◆ Where is your home? Country_____

   Town/State_____   Zip Code_____

◆ How many are in your party? _____adults _____children

◆ When you chose to go on today's boat trip, how important to you was each of the following

   activities in percentage terms (should total to 100%): touring/sightseeing_____%

   lunch/dinner_____% snorkeling_____% scuba_____% fishing_____% whale

   watching_____% other (please specify activity)_____%

◆ When you booked your Hawai`i trip, did you know that humpback whales would be in

   Hawaiian waters during your visit? ☐ Yes ☐ No

◆ If you did know that whales would be here, how much of a factor were the whales in your

   decision to come to Hawai`i? ☐ not a factor ☐ a small factor ☐ one of several important

   factors ☐ a very important factor

◆ When you chose to go on today's boat trip, how important to you was each of the following activities in percentage terms (should total to 100%): touring/sightseeing_____% lunch/dinner_____% snorkeling_____% scuba_____% fishing_____% whale watching_____% other (please specify activity)_____%

Tour Operator Survey

The "Whale Watching Survey" shown below was designed with assistance from representatives of both the ocean tour boat industry and Hawai`i state government. The survey was distributed to more than 100 ocean tour operators throughout Hawai`i in March 1999. The survey was accompanied by a cover letter and a fact sheet that explained the goals of the project and the purpose of the survey. Survey responses were tabulated and analyzed as discussed in Appendix A.

II
The Demand for Whalewatching at Stellwagen Bank National Marine Sanctuary

Porter Hoagland and Andrew E. Meeks
Marine Policy Center
Woods Hole Oceanographic Institution

II

The Demand for Whalewatching at Stellwagen Bank National Marine Sanctuary*

Porter Hoagland and Andrew E. Meeks

Marine Policy Center
Woods Hole Oceanographic Institution
Woods Hole, Massachusetts 02543

* This report was prepared under sponsorship of the U.S. Department of Commerce, National Oceanic and Atmospheric Administration, Ref. No. 4OCEAN602417 and the Marine Policy Center, WHOI. Comments and suggestions are welcome. Please contact the lead author at the above address or at phoagland@whoi.edu or 508-289-2867.

ACKNOWLEDGMENTS

We would like to thank several firms in the whalewatching industry for participating in and making possible the survey on which this report is based. These firms include Captain John Boats (Plymouth), Hyannis Whalewatcher (Barnstable), Captain Bill and Sons (Gloucester), the Dolphin Fleet (Provincetown), the New England Aquarium (Boston), the East India Cruise Company (Salem), Captain Mac's (Scituate), and the New England Whale Watch (Newburyport). We would also like to thank Rebecca Lawrence and Mary Schumacher for research assistance; Andy Beet and Heather Leslie for conducting surveys; Denise Jarvinen, Yoshi Kaoru, George Parsons, and Linwood Pendleton for suggestions and reviews; and Brad Barr and Peter Auster for research sponsorship.

TABLE OF CONTENTS

EXECUTIVE SUMMARY

Since its beginnings in the mid-1970s, whalewatching has grown tremendously to rank among the New England region's most important recreational industries, with gross sales revenues of roughly $21 million annually. In this report, we estimate the net economic "use" value (primarily consumer surplus) associated with whalewatching at the Stellwagen Bank National Marine Sanctuary. Although we do not develop a model that provides estimates of changes in net benefits associated with changes in environmental quality or with changes in levels of conflicting human uses, the results reported here nevertheless provide a starting point for an evaluation of the total economic value of the sanctuary.

We present the results of a survey of whalewatch trips during August of 1996. The majority of survey respondents are from the New England region, but more than one-third of those surveyed were vacationing from outside the region. More than two-thirds of vacationers (from New England and elsewhere) had planned to go on a whalewatch as a part of their vacation. When asked on their trip out about the importance of whalewatching relative to other activities on their vacation, vacationers reported that, on average, whalewatching represented more than one-third of the value of their vacation. Other highly ranked activities included going to the beach, shopping, going to museums, visiting relatives, and fishing.

We estimate that more than 860,000 whalewatches took place during 1996. Most whalewatching takes place in July and August, but the season stretches from April through October. The number of whales seen was reported as the most attractive feature of whalewatching. But the value of a whalewatching experience cannot be attributed solely to the viewing of whales, as "going on a boat trip" was also identified as an attractive feature. "Not enough whales seen" and "boats too far away" were cited as potential drawbacks.

Vacationers spend on average more than four days at vacation destinations in the New England region. We use this fact to handle the difficult "multiple site" issue that arises when the travel cost framework is employed. This issue relates to difficulties in factoring out the value of whalewatching from the total value of a vacation. We assume that, on a specific day, vacationers are traveling from their vacation destinations to go whalewatching only. Using a zonal travel cost approach, we find that decisions to go whalewatching are negatively related to travel costs and income but positively related to education level. The relationship between income and whalewatching appears counterintuitive, unless we hypothesize that higher income groups tend to "use" the whales in ways other than through commercial boat rides, say, by cruising on their own yachts. (An alternative model that utilizes data from each vacationer's home municipality suggests that whalewatching participation may, in fact, increase with income.)

Econometric estimation of the demand relationship leads us to conclude that, using a discount rate of 5 percent, the capitalized economic value of whalewatching is on the order of

$440 million. Consumer surplus per trip is about $26.00, which compares favorably with other studies of the value of environmental resources using similar techniques. Our estimate is slightly lower than one made a decade earlier. The most likely reason for this difference is our conservative approach to the multiple site issue. Finally, we note that whalewatching is a time-consuming activity that must compete with other modes of recreation. A high price elasticity of demand suggests that, for many consumers, there are close substitute activities, and, therefore, our consumer surplus estimates are not unexpected.

A separate unpublished study (Meeks 1996) finds that the rate of increase in whalewatching capacity has been fairly constant over the last few years. We would expect that whalewatching would grow with increasing economic growth, but there may be other factors, such as congestion, that limit the continued growth of the industry. If our analysis is correct, the demand for whalewatching should expand with increased education levels. This finding suggests that a policy of raising the level of education could help to maintain the growth of this particular form of "eco-tourism."

Keywords: whalewatching, marine recreational industries, Stellwagen Bank National Marine Sanctuary, economic value of marine recreation, economic value of marine sanctuaries

INTRODUCTION

Stellwagen Bank is an extraordinary marine environment that has economic value because it is rare. Stellwagen Bank's economic value can, in theory, be determined from an examination of the productive uses of the resources located on or in association with it, including fish, marine mammals, historic shipwrecks, among others (S&RD 1993). In economic parlance, the "demand" for Stellwagen Bank's environment can be "derived" from its contribution both to these economically productive processes and to the welfare of passive users (cf. Ellis and Fisher 1987).

In this report, we estimate the economic value associated with one important use of Stellwagen Bank: whalewatching. Since its beginnings in the mid-1970s, whalewatching has grown tremendously to rank among the New England region's most important recreational industries. Commercial whalewatching operations sailing to Stellwagen Bank operate out of eight "entry ports" distributed along the north and south shores of the Massachusetts coastline. Figure 1 compares the size of the whalewatch industry, in terms of gross revenues or expenditures (on a logarithmic scale), with the size of other industries and activities in Massachusetts.

The kind of comparison made in Figure 1 gives us a sense of the scale of various activities. However, the units employed are more a measure of economic impacts than of the net benefits from each activity. In terms of understanding the economic value of an industry or an activity to the economy, we need to look more precisely at the demand and supply of the relevant goods and services.

We employ a traditional method for estimating total economic "use" value at Stellwagen Bank. This kind of value can be useful to marine resource managers who wish to consider the opportunity costs of the displacement of whalewatching by other uses. At Stellwagen Bank, activities that have some potential for displacing whalewatching include environmental impacts from the sewage disposal outfall pipe extending out from Boston Harbor, the disposal of dredged materials in or near the boundary of the sanctuary, and some types of commercial or recreational fishing activities.

Ideally, marine resource managers would like to have a method for estimating marginal effects such as the loss of net benefits associated with whalewatching due to incremental increases in other mutually exclusive uses of the ocean. For several reasons, we are unable to estimate marginal effects directly in this application. First, it is not clear that changes in other uses of the ocean have immediate, measurable adverse impacts on the demand for whalewatching. Second, general environmental effects that are unrelated to human uses, such as natural variations in food sources, may be so large as to obscure any human impacts. Third, the economic models that have been developed to measure marginal effects may not be appropriate to this specific case. (This latter point will be explained in greater detail below.[1])

Although we do not develop a model that provides estimates of changes in net benefits associated with changes in environmental quality or with changes in levels of conflicting human uses, the results reported here nevertheless provide a starting point for an evaluation of the total economic value of the sanctuary.

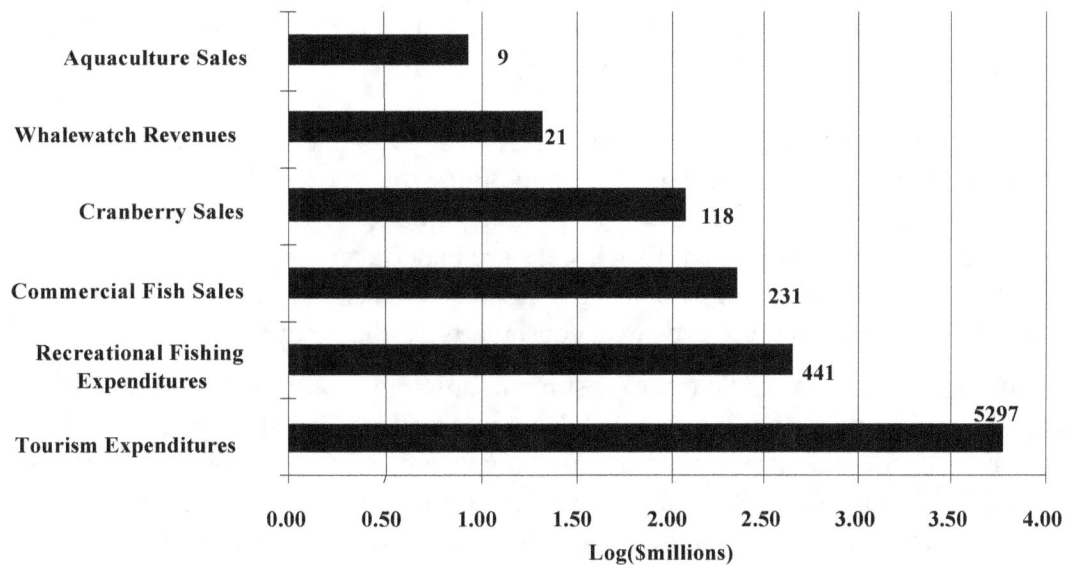

Figure 1: Estimated gross revenues or expenditures for industries and other activities in Massachusetts in 1996. Note that the units are measured in logarithms of millions of dollars. Gross revenues are shown for aquaculture (1995 data; Spatz et al. 1996), whalewatching (this report), cranberry production (NASS 1997), and commercial fish landings (NMFS 1997). Recreational fishing expenditures were estimated as the product of an estimated number of 1994 saltwater anglers (NMFS 1995) times a 1991 estimate of average expenditures per angler (DoC and DoI 1993), which was revised downward to reduce sources of double counting. Tourism expenditures were estimated as the sum of domestic tourist expenditures in coastal counties plus a percentage of total foreign tourist expenditures (Robert 1997). Tourism expenditures were reduced by the sum of recreational fishing expenditures and whalewatching revenues.

---

[1] With a credible estimate of aggregate demand for whalewatching, it is possible to estimate changes in net benefits through factors, such as increased regulation of whalewatching, that may cause shifts in the supply of whalewatching trips.

GENERAL METHODOLOGY

There are several economic methodologies that can be used to obtain estimates of the economic value of a marine area (Freeman 1996; Hoagland et al. 1995). The relevant method depends upon both the purpose of the study and the particular characteristics of the site.

Our main purpose is to develop a deeper understanding of the value that society places on the presence of whales at Stellwagen Bank. This value can be divided roughly into two components: use value and passive value. In this study we estimate the use value of whales found on Stellwagen Bank. Such an estimate is important because it allows us to compare the economic significance of whalewatching with other potentially conflicting or mutually exclusive uses of the marine environment. We update and expand upon an earlier study of the use value of whalewatching out of Gloucester in 1986 (Day 1987).

Primarily because of limits on the financial resources available for the study, we do not attempt to estimate passive value. Extensive work involving the testing of hypothetical market questions using focus groups and other costly steps is required to develop credible estimates of passive values (Hanemann 1994). Even if such steps are undertaken, the practice of estimating passive use values can be highly controversial (Diamond and Hausman 1994). As such, the use value estimates that we report here clearly are a conservative estimate of total economic value.

We employ a traditional zonal travel cost methodology (ZTCM) in this study. The advantages of ZTCM are its simplicity, minimal data requirements, and solid grounding in economic theory. Other methods of estimating use value were considered but rejected due to the characteristics of the application. For example, random utility approaches, which are employed to analyze choices among sites and changes in site attributes, may be inappropriate for the following reason: although there are several "entry ports" from which individuals can embark to go whalewatching, in this case the resource that they are "using" (whales—mostly humpbacks—on Stellwagen Bank) is identical across ports. As a result, there is little variability in the recreational experience across ports (and none with respect to the resource itself).[2] Further, the results of our surveys suggest that individuals usually do not choose among entry ports on the basis of anything other than travel cost.

A ZTCM model can be estimated with data from surveys of the users on site or from a mail survey. Based upon the results of a test survey of users on site, we found that a large proportion of whalewatchers are from outside the New England region. As a result, we decided to survey the users on site. If we had conducted a mail survey of users in New England, we expected that we would have been unable to capture demand from the tourist and vacationer

---

[2] Meeks (1996) finds that whalewatch firms can be described as operating in a competitive market offering an undifferentiated product.

components.[3] Further, we expected that a mail survey of the nation, at considerable cost, would be unlikely to result in usable response rates.

---

[3] We need to make some restrictive assumptions about the vacationer component, which we describe below.

APPLICATION

Figure 2 is a map of the coast of Massachusetts showing the location of each of eight whalewatching "entry ports" (Newburyport, Salem, Gloucester, Boston, Scituate, Plymouth, Hyannis, and Provincetown) and their geographic relationship to the Stellwagen Bank National Marine Sanctuary. The number of whalewatch operators is identified at the location of each entry port. In 1996, there were a total of 16 operators in the region, each operating from 1 to 4 boats (Table 1).

Table 1: **Stellwagen Bank Whalewatch Firms and Number of Vessels (as of 1996 season)**

Entry Port	Firms	No. of Boats
Gloucester	Cape Ann Whale Watch	1
	Captain Bill and Sons	2
	Seven Seas Whale Watching	1
	Atlantic Yankee Whale Watch	3
Newburyport	New England Whale Watch	1
Salem	East India Cruise Company	1
Boston	A.C. Cruise Lines	1
	Boston Harbor Whale Watch	1
	New England Aquarium	1
Scituate	Captain Mac's	1
Plymouth	Andy-Lynn Whale Watch	1
	Captain John's	3-7
Barnstable	Hyannis Whale Watcher	1
Provincetown	Dolphin Fleet	3
	Portuguese Princess Whale Watch	1
	Provincetown Whale Watch	1
TOTAL		23-27

Our first step was the drafting of a survey instrument. We conducted test surveys during 24-25 July 1996 in both Plymouth and Hyannis. The survey instrument was revised and eight surveys were conducted during 14-28 August 1996. Tabulated results of the revised surveys for each of the entry ports are available from the lead author. Figure 3 displays the distribution of the total number of respondents per seaport (n=271).

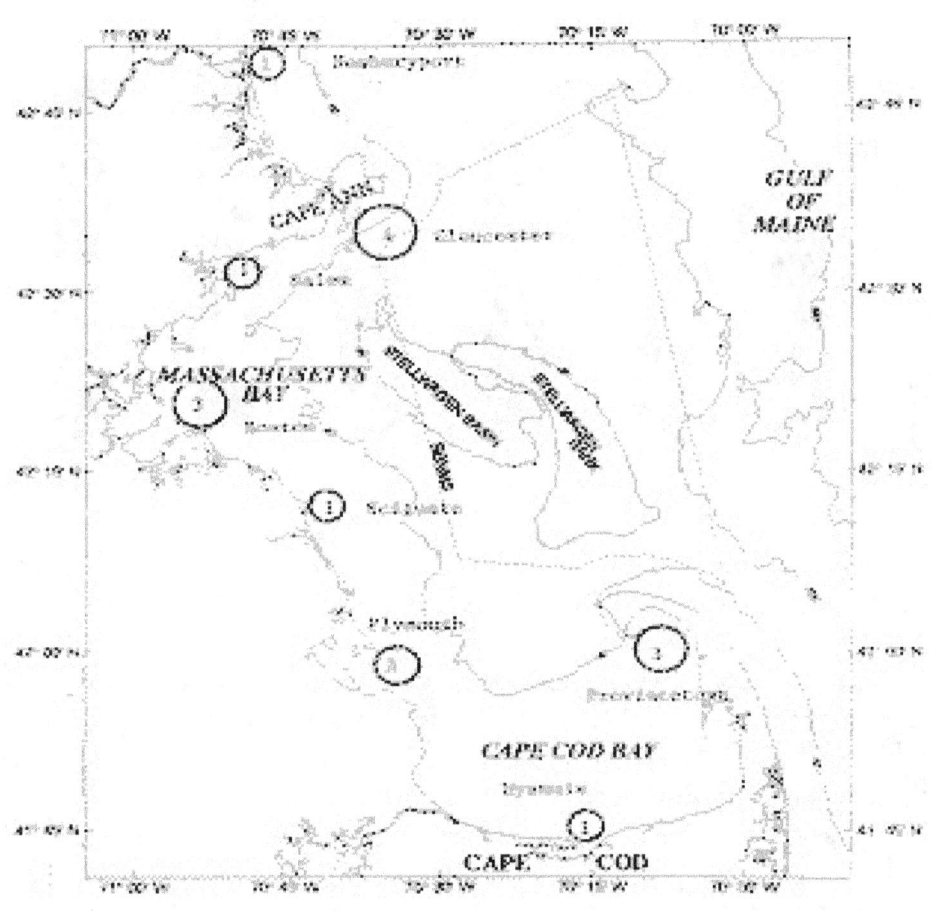

Figure 2: Location of whalewatch "entry ports" and number of firms operating out of each port in 1996. Source: personal communications with whalewatch operators and Barr (1996).

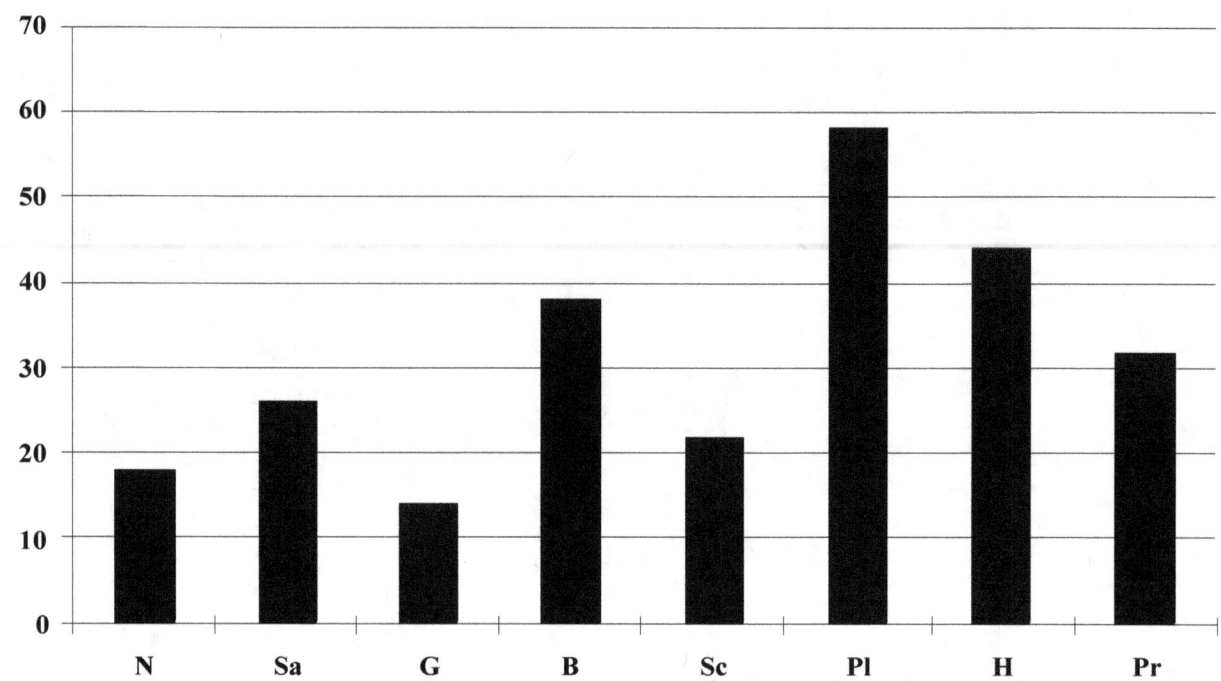

Figure 3: Distribution of survey responses across entry ports. Key: N=Newburyport; Sa=Salem; G=Gloucester; B=Boston; Sc=Scituate; Pl=Plymouth; H=Hyannis; Pr=Provincetown

People come to watch whales at Stellwagen Bank from all parts of the world. Very few people go whalewatching more than once a year.[4] Figure 4 shows the geographic distribution of respondents from our surveys at each entry port. The majority of whalewatchers are from the United States (especially New England), but our sample identified visitors from Europe and Japan as well. Across the sample, 32 percent of the visitors came from outside the region.

Figure 5 looks more closely at the extent to which vacationers have planned a whalewatch trip as a part of their vacation. For each entry port, Figure 5 breaks down the responses into the following categories: (1) day trips from home; (2) vacationers who have planned a whalewatch as part of their vacation; (3) vacationers who decided to go on a whalewatch spontaneously; and (4) vacationers who did not respond. More than two-thirds of the vacationers we surveyed had planned to go on a whalewatch as a part of their vacation.

---

[4]In fact, we believe that few go whalewatching more than once in a lifetime.

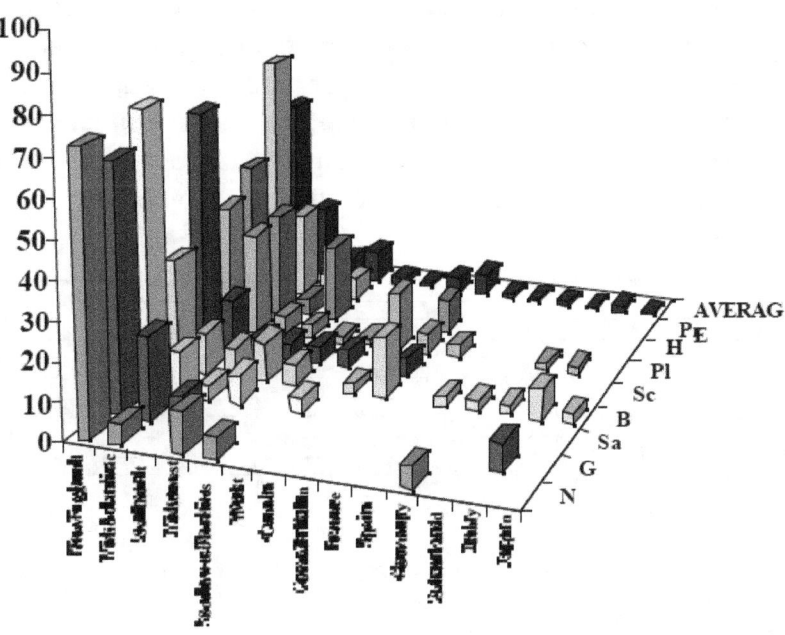

Figure 4: The geographic distribution of respondents across entry ports. Bars represent the percent of total respondents.

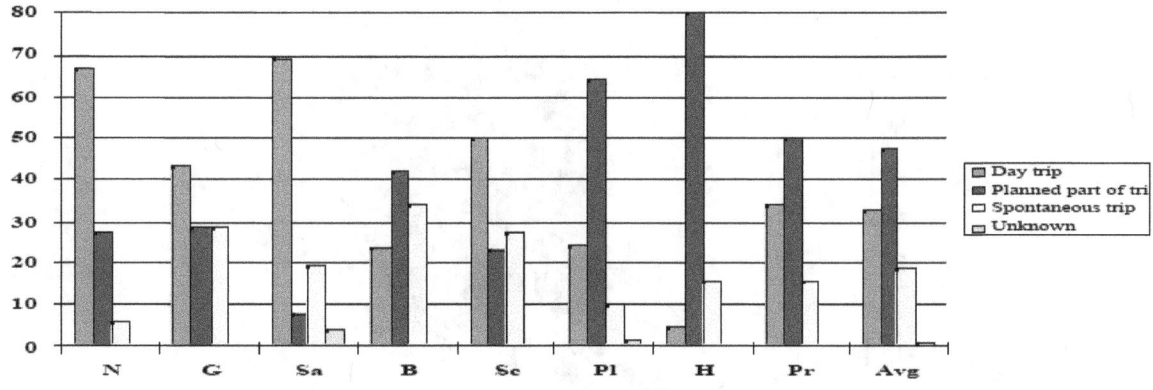

Figure 5: Whalewatch trips by type across entry ports. Bars represent the percentage of respondents at each port. The leftmost bars are the percentage of respondents traveling from home. The other bars break down trips made by vacationers into planned, spontaneous, or unknown.

Figure 6 shows, for vacationers at each entry port, the average percent importance of going on a whalewatch relative to the importance of participating in other activities during a vacation. This figure shows that, on average, vacationers perceive whalewatching to be a very important part of their trip (more than 37 percent over the entire sample). We note that, because surveys were administered during the whalewatch trip, this response could be biased upwards due to the immediacy of the whalewatch relative to other vacation activities.

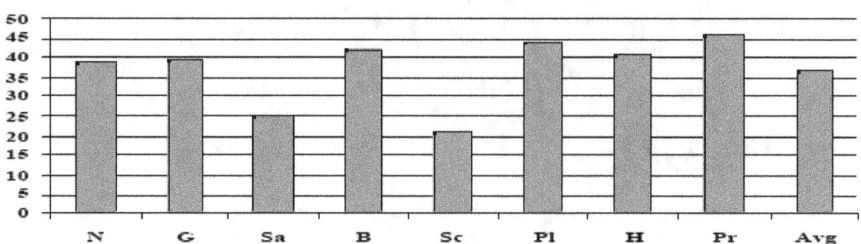

Figure 6: *Average percent importance relative to all vacation activities of going on a whalewatch to vacationers at each entry port.*

Figure 7 shows the participation of vacationers in other activities. Each respondent could pick one or more activities, and Figure 7 compares the activities across entry ports in terms of total participation (each activity is expressed as a percent of total responses). Among the activities recording the highest participation are going to the beach, shopping, going to museums, visiting relatives, and fishing.

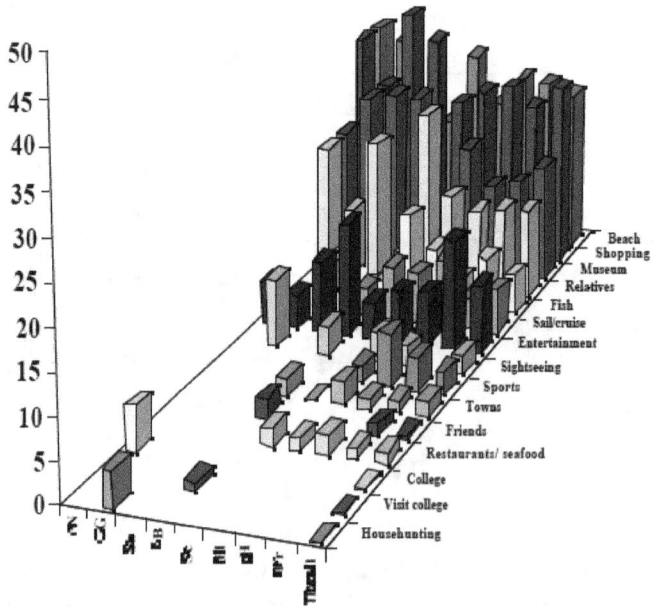

Figure 7: *Importance to vacationers of vacation activities other than whalewatching across entry ports. Bars represent the relative percent importance of activities (not including the importance of whalewatching).*

Respondents also were asked about those features that make a whalewatch attractive. Again, each respondent could choose one or more responses. Responses are displayed in Figure 8, showing each category as a percent of total responses. As shown in Figure 8, except in the case of Scituate, the "number of whales seen" received a higher number of responses as an attractive feature than the other features. An interesting finding is that "going on a boat trip" is a highly rated attractive feature of whalewatching, suggesting that an estimate of the value of a whalewatching experience cannot be attributed solely to the viewing of whales.[5] Also important are the "number of species seen" and the "naturalist interpretations.[6]

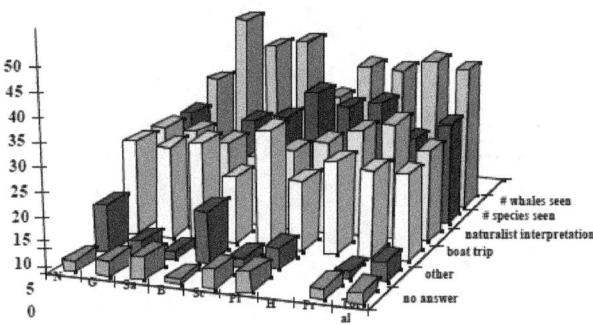

Figure 8: "Attractive features" of whalewatching as reported by respondents at each entry port. Bars represent the percent of total responses.

Figure 9 presents the responses to a question about drawbacks to a whalewatch. Many people did not respond to the question. This reaction may have occurred because the survey was distributed on the trip out to see the whales, and respondents may have had little basis for answering the question. Those that did respond identified "not enough whales seen" and "whales too far away" as drawbacks. On the Salem trips, the presence of other whalewatching boats was cited as a drawback more frequently than the other responses.

---

[5] Even so, we consider time spent on the trip as an opportunity cost.

[6] In a random sample of greater Boston area residents, Elasmar (1996) finds that 86.4% of respondents prefer having a certified naturalist on board a whalewatching boat. Elasmar (1996) also found that 77% of respondents would prefer a naturalist specifically trained about the Stellwagen Bank National Marine Sanctuary.

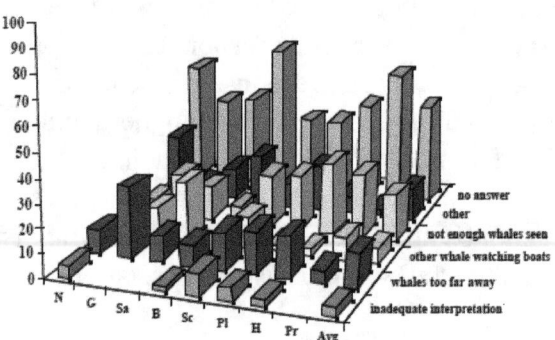

Figure 9: *Drawbacks to whalewatching as reported by respondents at each entry port. Bars represent the percent of total responses.*

MODEL DEVELOPMENT

According to economic theory, an individual person's utility depends upon the consumption of goods and services, which may include visits to a recreational site—such as a trip to Stellwagen Bank to watch whales. Each individual chooses an optimal affordable bundle of goods. Demand is the result of a choice to consume a positive level of some good, and it depends—in part—upon the price of the relevant good. The relevant price of a whalewatch trip is travel cost, which is calculated from mileage costs, time costs, and ticket prices.

A demand relationship can be estimated using data from a survey of individuals. The area under an aggregate demand curve is a measure of the benefits of whalewatching on Stellwagen Bank. Figure 10 depicts a stylized model of the demand and supply of whalewatching. Our study provides an estimate of area A in the diagram. We expect that the supply curve is fairly flat, reflecting the ease with which firms can enter and exit the whalewatching business, using simple conversions of party fishing boats, and the overall competitiveness of the industry (Terkla 1990). Thus B is expected to be small, although some of the best operators may earn rents in the short run. Meeks (1996) finds that innovations created to differentiate one operator's "product" from others' are rapidly adopted by the other operators.

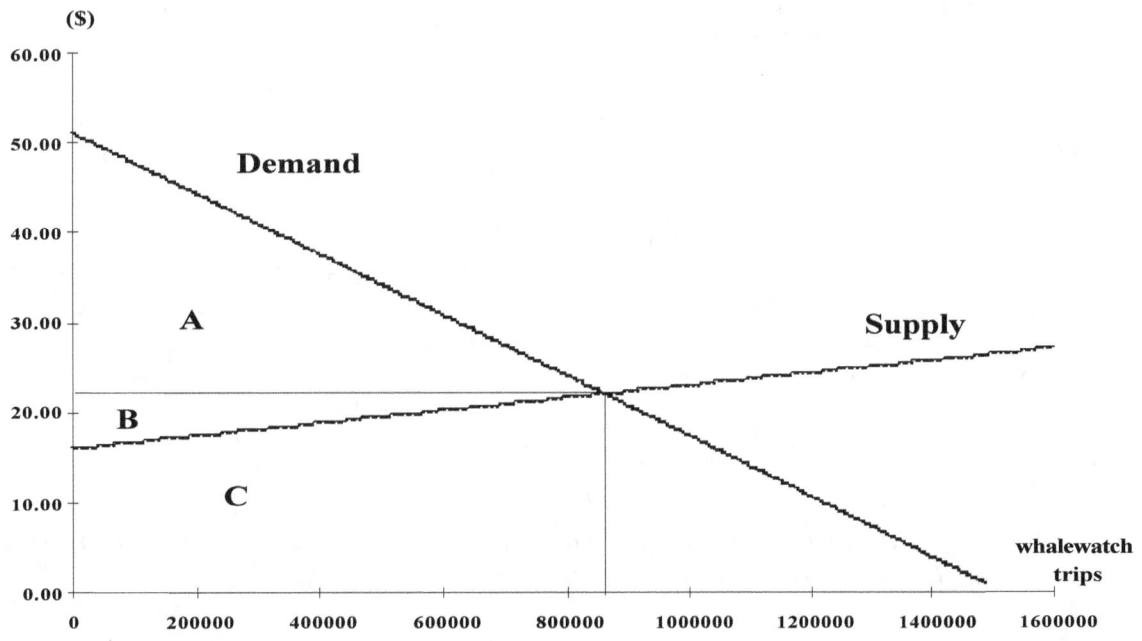

Figure 10: *A stylized model of the demand and supply of whalewatching trips in any year. Area A represents consumers surplus, which is what we aim to estimate in this report. Area B represents producers surplus, which, because the supply curve is very flat, we expect to be small. Area A+B is net economic value. Area C represents the aggregate cost of the whalewatching activity. Area B+C is the gross revenue from whalewatching.*

We can readily estimate the size of area B+C as a product of the estimated number of whalewatchers in any particular year and the average price of a ticket. Area B+C is a measure of the gross revenues from whalewatching, and it gives us an idea of the size of the industry, but it is not a measure of the net benefits of whalewatching. Figure 11 presents our method for estimating the total number of whalewatch visits in 1996. The season begins in April when the humpback whales move into the area and the weather becomes mild enough to take passengers out to see the whales. A small peak in visits occurs in May-June associated with school field trips. The highest number of visits occurs during the summer vacation months of July-August. Finally, the business usually winds down in October. We estimate the box shown in Figure 10 that surrounds the July-August peak. This box is calculated by estimating the capacity of the whole whalewatch fleet (75% of the total number of seats) times the number of trips taken during July and August. We estimate a total of 863,570 trips in 1996.

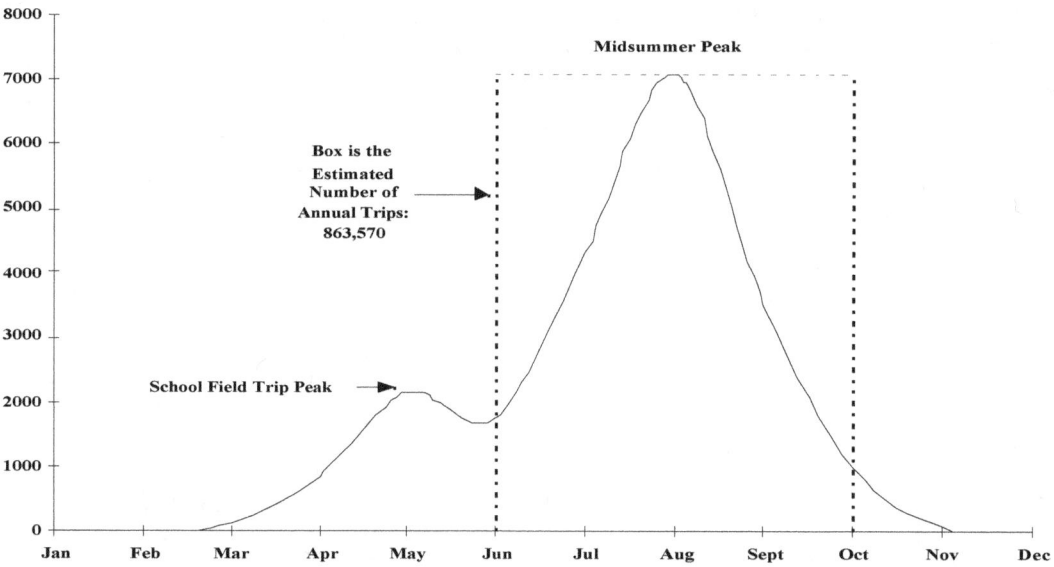

Figure 11: *Approximate distribution of whalewatch trips across the year. Note the two peaks. The size of the peak corresponding to school field trips in 1996 is unknown.*

The ZTCM involves an hypothesis that decisions by individuals to go whalewatching depend upon the cost of travel from their residences to an entry port. Travel cost is an aggregate cost composed of (1) the roundtrip cost of driving to an entry port and back, (2) the price of whalewatch tickets, and (3) the opportunity cost of time spent traveling and whalewatching. The

70

likelihood that an individual decides to go whalewatching also may depend upon her age, education level, income, or possibly other "socioeconomic" variables.

There are six basic assumptions employed in the ZTCM. We list these assumptions here and discuss them in greater detail as we proceed through a description of the model.

1. *Travel is costly, and costs increase with distance.* This assumption clearly holds in our application.

2. *The sole purpose of a trip is to visit a specific site.* In most cases, this assumption does not hold in our application because many whalewatchers are vacationing or traveling to an entry port to do things other than just whalewatching. We discuss our approach for dealing with this problem below.

3. *All visits involve the same length of time at the site.* This assumption seems reasonable, because most whalewatch tours are of the same length (about 4 hours).

4. *Whalewatchers respond to changes in ticket prices in the same way that they respond to changes in travel costs.* This assumption appears to hold, as long as whalewatchers have a clear conception of their costs of travel.

5. *A whalewatcher's wage is a good measure of the opportunity costs of time.* This assumption is weak in our application because many whalewatchers are below the age of employment, retired, or on paid vacation from work. We discuss our approach to this issue below.

6. *No alternative recreation sites of the same type exist.* Broadly speaking, alternative recreation sites of the same type, namely whales on Stellwagen Bank, do not exist. Vacationers may choose between entry ports, but the relevant product, a "whalewatch trip," is virtually identical across ports. Thus we believe that this assumption holds in our application.

Our application of the ZTCM involves the calculation of a "participation rate" and a travel cost from each "zone of origin" to an entry port. In a typical application, zones of origin are constructed as concentric circles focused on an entry port. This method is the one employed by Day (1987) in a travel cost analysis of the benefits of whalewatching in Gloucester in 1986.[7] The concentric circle method can involve error, because the travel costs for individuals from any zone may vary considerably within that zone. We reduce this source of error by identifying each

---

[7]We compare our results with those of Day (1987) below.

of 33 counties in New England as a distinct zone (cf. Hufschmidt 1983).[8] Each county is an "observation" in the model.

Our most important piece of data from the surveys is the home or vacation residence of whalewatchers. We calculate a participation rate (which might be zero) for each zone from observed participation from that zone (Grandstaff and Dixon 1986). The participation rate is calculated as follows:

$$PRATE_i = \frac{\left(\dfrac{w_i}{\sum\limits_{i=1}^{33} w_i}\right) \cdot W}{POP_i}$$

where w_i is the observed number of whalewatchers in county i, W is the estimated total annual number of whalewatch "visits" in the region (i.e., 863,570 trips), and POP_i is the population of county i. Thus $PRATE_i$ gives us an estimate of the proportion of county i's total population that went whalewatching in 1996. The participation rate is the dependent variable in the models we estimate in this report ("DPRATE" or "RPRATE," defined below).

One concern is the treatment of visitors from outside the region. Figure 4, above, displays the geographic distribution of respondents from our sample. Although most of the respondents are from the 33 counties in the New England region, a considerable proportion of the respondents are from outside the region, including some visitors from as far away as Europe and Japan. Figure 5 displays the distribution at each entry port of individuals who are making day trips from home compared to individuals who are vacationing in the region. If we estimate the travel cost from very distant locations, the estimated benefits of whalewatching could be very large. Such an approach could be a source of error in the model if visitors from distant locations are traveling to New England to do things other than just whalewatching. In many applications, these "outliers" are dropped from the model. However, on average, visitors from outside the region are staying at vacation destinations inside the region for more than 4 days. (This number varies considerably across entry ports, as shown in Figure 12.) As a result, we construct two general formulations. In the first, we treat all vacationers (even those from New England) as if they reside in the county where they are vacationing.[9] We refer to this as the "destination model." In the second formulation, we assume that all residents from New England counties are

---

[8]Initially, we had hoped to identify individual towns as distinct zones. The data collection needed to estimate a model at the town level proved to be too labor-intensive for this application.

[9]This too is a potential source of error because the socioeconomic characteristics of the vacationers may not necessarily match the median or average socioeconomic characteristics of the county in which they are vacationing. We have made a subjective decision to accept this source of error.

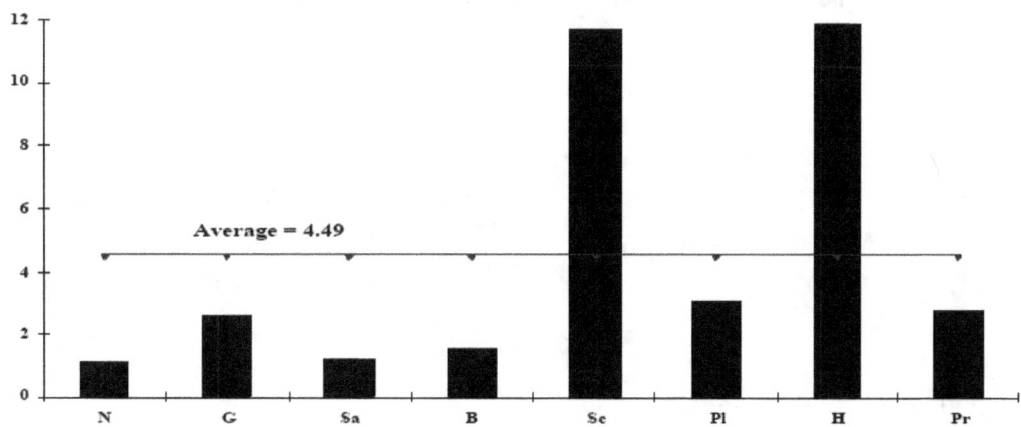

Figure 12: *The average number of days spent by vacationers at their vacation destinations. Data is arranged by entry port. The global average is 4.49 days.*

traveling from their home counties-- even if they are vacationing elsewhere in New England. All vacationers from outside New England are assumed to be travelling from their vacation destination. We refer to this as the "regional model."

The approach of treating vacationers as New England "residents" helps to ameliorate the multiple site problem. In essence, we are assuming that all participants are making day trips from either their home or their vacation destination just to go whalewatching. Recall that, on average, more than two-thirds of the vacationers planned to make whalewatching a part of their vacation (return to Figure 5).

Data on average or median level socioeconomic characteristics are collected for each zone. We compile county-level data on population, median income ("INCOME"), the percentage of county population with a college education ("COLLEGE"), and the percentage of county population above the age of 18 ("ADULT") from the statistical summaries published on the internet from the 1990 U.S. census by the U.S. Bureau of Census (BoC 1996). Table 2 summarizes descriptive statistics about these variables.

Table 2: Descriptive statistics concerning the model variables. All variables were converted to natural logarithms prior to estimation. "DPRATE" and "RPRATE" represent participation rates and "DTC" and "RTC" represent travel costs for the "destination" and "regional" models, respectively.

VARIABLE	MEAN	STANDARD DEVIATION	MINIMUM	MAXIMUM
EPRATE	0.0945	0.2502	0.00	1.2855
RPRATE	0.0940	0.1789	0.00	0.8264
Income ($)	36897.30	5358.82	29399.00	49891.00
College (% of pop.)	15.67	2.91	11.00	23.00
Adult (% of pop.)	76.88	1.87	74.00	81.00
DTC5 ($)	40.70	8.64	28.87	62.84
DTC10 ($)	47.25	10.51	32.12	76.04
DTC25 ($)	66.40	16.66	41.85	115.65
DTC33 ($)	76.62	20.01	47.05	136.77
DTC40 ($)	98.32	27.21	58.08	181.65
RTC10 ($)	30.93	13.19	4.08	61.66
RTC15 ($)	43.12	18.96	5.86	90.15
RTC25 ($)	49.63	22.07	6.81	105.35
RTC33 ($)	63.44	28.71	8.84	137.64

Next, we calculate a total travel cost variable ("DTC__" or "RTC__") by employing the following assumptions. To approximate driving costs, we multiply roundtrip travel distances from each county center to each entry port by the U.S. Office of Naval Research "negotiated government rate" of $0.31/mile. Roundtrip travel distances from a town closest to the center of each county to each of the eight entry ports were obtained from DeLorme's "CyberRouter".[10] This cost is divided by the average number of individual whalewatchers in a group (3.82 across the full sample) to obtain an estimate of the driving costs per whalewatcher. We approximate travel times from each county by summing (1) the total travel distance divided by 48 mph[11] and (2) the length of an average whalewatch cruise at each entry port. We multiply the travel time estimate by proportions (ranging from 5 to 50 percent) of the relevant "median wage" to determine opportunity "time values" of travel.[12] We use an average whalewatching ticket price of $24 per person. Finally, we sum the driving costs, the opportunity cost of travel, and the cost of a ticket to obtain an estimate of the total travel cost for each whalewatcher.

The calculation of an opportunity time value of travel is one potential source of concern. The U.S. Bureau of Census does not report a county-level wage rate. We calculate a county-level "median wage" rate by dividing the county median annual income by 2000 hours. Note that the Census Bureau's median income statistic is compiled from all sources of income (not just "work related" income), so this calculation may overestimate the opportunity cost of taking time off to go whalewatching.

A second issue is the assumption that those who go whalewatching are in fact incurring lost opportunities to earn wages or, alternatively, are foregoing other activities that, on the margin, are valued at the median wage rate. Our survey results suggest that large numbers of whalewatchers are on vacation and are not taking time off from work (return to Figure 4). Thus we suspect that the opportunity cost faced by most whalewatchers is substantially below the wage rate.

There is little consensus in the literature on the selection of an appropriate opportunity cost rate. McKean *et al.* (1995) find significant differences in opportunity time values between those who trade off time for income and those who do not. Their solution to this problem is to separate individuals into these two classes, and to estimate appropriate opportunity time values for each class. Other studies adopt the simpler approach of selecting a proportion of the "median wage" rate, usually about one-third of the median wage, and applying this to all individuals in the sample. We follow the latter approach, preferring, in the end, a proportion of the "median wage" rate (5 percent) that is smaller than that used in a typical ZTCM study. (Nevertheless, we run the model also at rates of 10, 25, 33, and 50 percent to demonstrate its sensitivity to the choice of an opportunity cost rate.) Our justification for selecting a smaller proportion is threefold: (1) a high proportion of the sample includes individuals who are retired,

---

[10] Found at: **http://www.delorme.com/cybermaps/route.asp**.

[11] All entry ports are connected to counties by easily accessible major highways. An average highway speed is reduced to account for traffic congestion and connections to the highways on smaller routes.

[12] We examine the sensitivity of the estimates to changes in the opportunity time value of travel below.

on vacation, or below the age of employment; (2) our median wage estimate is derived from a median income figure that is an overestimate of employment income; and (3) whalewatchers may "enjoy" taking a boat trip, thereby reducing the net opportunity cost of time. In practice, it may be possible to select the proportion by calibrating the model such that it predicts the same number of total whalewatch visits as those observed empirically.[13]

Another important assumption concerns our estimate of the distance traveled from each county center to the relevant entry port. We assume that whalewatchers always go to the nearest entry port. This statement is true in general but does not always hold in specific cases. One approach to this problem is to estimate first a demand relationship for each entry port, and then to aggregate demands over all ports. Unfortunately, our survey did not obtain observations of participation from enough counties at each entry port to permit estimation of demand for each port.[14]

---

[13] This technique works only if we know the appropriate model specification in advance. For example, ordinary least squares, tobit, and poisson models are likely to result in different predictions of the number of whalewatch participants.

[14] We attempted to construct a "weighted" travel cost variable that reflected the distribution of visits from each county across all potential entry ports. In practice, the distribution was heavily weighted in favor of the closest entry port.

RESULTS

We estimate demand for both the "destination" and "regional" models using a log-linear ordinary least squares technique. The general form is:

$$\ln(\_PRATE_i) = \ln(cons\tan t) + \beta_1 \ln(travel\cos t_i) + \beta_2 \ln(income_i) + \beta_3 \ln(college_i) + \beta_4 \ln(adult_i) + \varepsilon_i$$

Parameter estimates for the two models (using a travel cost based upon the opportunity cost rate of 10 percent of the median wage) are presented in Table 3. Both models were corrected for potential heteroskedastic inefficiency, which is common in zonal travel cost models (Bowes and Loomis 1980). Under both specifications, the travel cost parameter is negative and significant. This result is in accord with economic theory and is to be expected from the construction of the model, particularly with a low opportunity cost of time rate.

Table 3: **Comparison of results from log-linear OLS estimations. All variables were converted to natural logarithms prior to estimation. Standard errors are reported in parentheses. Asterisks indicate the level of significance (*=10%; **=5%; ***=1%).**

OCT=10%	*Destination* MODEL	REGIONAL MODEL
Dependent Variable	DPRATE	RPRATE
Constant	100.66*	35.49
	(54.22)	(33.49)
Travel Cost	-7.90**	-2.26***
	(3.05)	(0.60)
Income	-4.20***	-2.79**
	(1.18)	(1.21)
College	5.03***	3.39***
	(0.66)	(0.88)
Adult	-9.09	-1.13
	(10.14)	(7.05)
R^2	0.67	0.69

The parameter describing the proportion of a county's population with a college education is positive and significant in both models. This result makes sense because we expect that a higher education level is correlated with a propensity to observe nature and the environment.

The median income parameter is negative and significant in both models. This result appears counterintuitive. Normally, we might expect to see higher income levels correlated with a propensity to observe nature and the environment. One interpretation is that whalewatching may be more of a low income-type recreation. According to this interpretation, higher income-types either are not very interested in whalewatching or perhaps they tend to go see whales using their own yachts. An alternative explanation relates to the issue of assuming that vacationers are "residing" in their vacation destination counties. If these counties tend to have lower median incomes that do not reflect the income status of the vacationers, then the results might be biased.[15]

To test the latter explanation, we constructed a separate data set that uses socioeconomic data from each vacationer's home municipalities. We continue to measure travel costs from the vacation destinations. Using this model, we find that increases in income do result in higher levels of whalewatch participation. The model does not explain very much of the variation in the data, so we do not report the results here or use it to estimate demand.[16] However, this result suggests that our concerns about bias have some merit.

The parameter estimates describing the proportion of each county's population above the age of 18 are negative in both models. This result is suggestive that whalewatching appeals to a younger audience, but the parameter estimates were insignificant.[17]

Parameter estimates from the models are used to predict the participation rate from each county when the values of its variables are plugged in. To analyze the response of participation rates to changes in travel cost, the fee (i.e., the whalewatch ticket price) is increased in a step-by-step process, and a new participation rate is calculated at each step. (The values of the other independent variables do not change. The sum of the constant term and the products of these other variables with their parameter estimates define a choke price for each county's demand.) At each level of the ticket price, the relevant participation rate from each county can be converted

---

[15]This source of bias could affect the other parameter estimates similarly.

[16] This model is a subject of ongoing research.

[17] The alternative model, using data from vacationer home municipalities, finds that whalewatch participation *increases* with increasing age. Again, the parameter is insignificant.

into an estimated participation level (number of whalewatch trips). Trips are summed across all counties to determine the aggregate demand for whalewatch trips at each price level.

Many studies have used some variant of an ordinary least squares (OLS) model to estimate the parameters.[18] For example, Day (1987) transforms a nonlinear multiplicative model by logarithms to estimate zonal travel cost by OLS. To run a log-linear OLS model, we omit those observations with a zero participation rate. Parameter estimates derived from the model with those counties that recorded a positive participation rate can be used to estimate participation rates for all 33 of the counties in the sample. Figure 13 displays the resulting aggregate demand curve using an opportunity cost of 5 percent in the regional model. The curve appears relatively elastic over the range of small increases from the prevailing ticket price. Because whalewatch participants are likely to have a wide variety of alternative recreational activities, we expect trips to decline rapidly with any price increases. For the higher range of prices, the curve becomes much more inelastic, suggesting that participants from some counties are willing to pay a considerable amount to go whalewatching.

---

[18] As noted earlier, our approach of using New England counties as observations resulted in a substantial number of counties with a zero participation rate. A conventional way of handling this issue is to treat participation rate as a censored dependent variable (with the censoring at zero), applying a tobit regression. Under this interpretation, negative participation rates can exist in theory but are not observed in practice. The practical interpretation of "negative participation" in a whalewatch is problematic. Our attempt to employ a tobit model resulted in estimates of negative participation from all counties, and, therefore, we abandoned this model. Another approach is to treat the participation rate as "count data," applying a poisson regression. Count data models are appropriate where the dependent variable is recorded in integer values. In order to estimate this model, the participation rates would need to be rounded to the nearest integer. We attempted this approach as well, discovering a very good fit with the data. However, the model was a poor predictor of the total number of whalewatch trips in a season, and, therefore, we also abandoned this model.

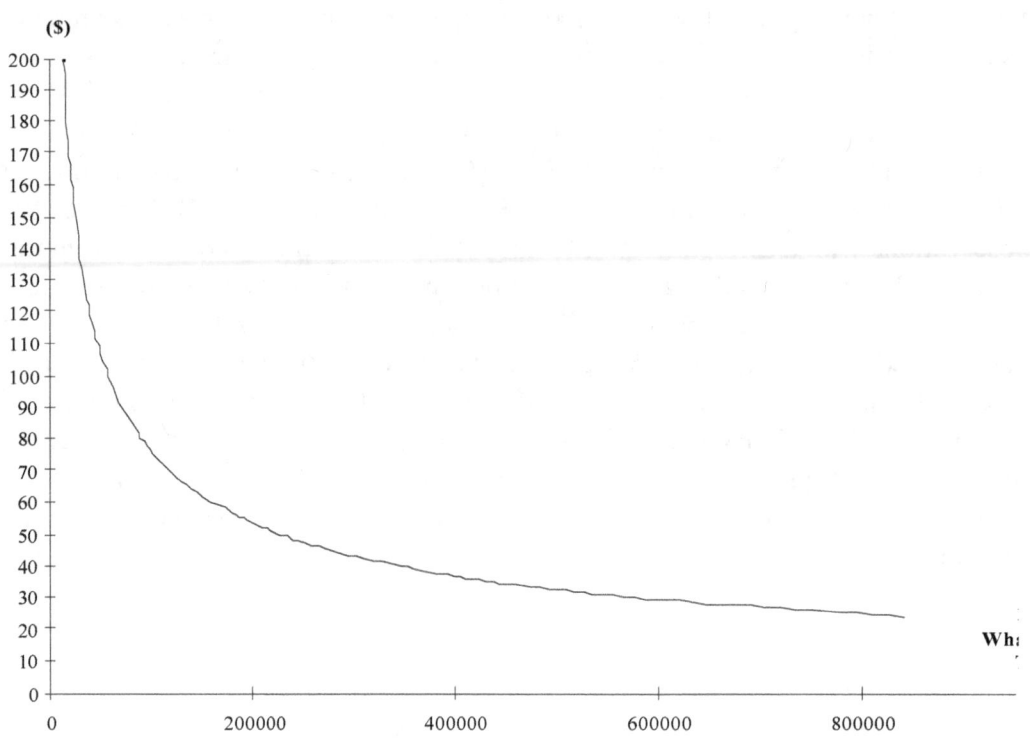

Figure 13: *Estimated demand for whalewatching at Stellwagen Bank in 1996: OLS log-log model. (Note that the choke price is not shown in this graph.)*

In Table 4, we present the results of a sensitivity analysis focusing on changes in the opportunity cost of time rate. For each model, across opportunity cost rates ranging from 5 to 50%, we report: (1) the predicted total annual number of whalewatch trips; (2) the average consumer surplus per trip (the consumer surplus estimate divided by the total annual number of trips); and (3) the capitalized present value of consumer surplus (in millions of dollars), at discount rates of 2, 5, and 10%. Estimates vary considerably depending upon the model employed and the assumed opportunity cost of time (OCT). Because the regional model gives us a better sense of actual participation from counties in New England and results in a slightly better estimate of total visits, we prefer estimates from this model. However, because of the low opportunity cost of time observed in the sample, we prefer the estimates developed using a 5 percent opportunity cost.

Table 4: Comparison of model results at different levels of the opportunity cost of time ("OCT"). Values reported include the predicted number of trips, the average consumer surplus ("CS") per trip, and the net present value ("NPV") at three discount rates (in millions of dollars). Our preferred estimate is the OCT of 5% for the Regional Model.

	Destination Model				Regional Model				
OCT	10	25	33	50	5	10	25	33	50
Predicted Trips	801287	816588	819156	822718	841307	840617	841224	841760	841149
CS/Trip	5.64	8.24	9.73	13.02	25.93	31.32	47.21	55.50	72.65
NPV (2%)	226	336	399	535	1091	1316	1986	2336	3055
NPV (5%)	90	135	159	214	436	526	794	934	1222
NPV (10%)	45	67	80	107	281	263	397	467	611

Average consumer surplus per trip ranges from a low of $5.64 (Destination Model, OCT = 10%) to a high of $72.65 (Regional Model, OCT = 50%). Our preferred estimate is $25.93 (Regional Model, OCT = 5%) per trip. In Figure 14, we show how average consumer surplus per trip varies with changes in the opportunity cost rate for both models. The average consumer surplus per trip estimate appears comparable with estimates from other studies (Table 5).

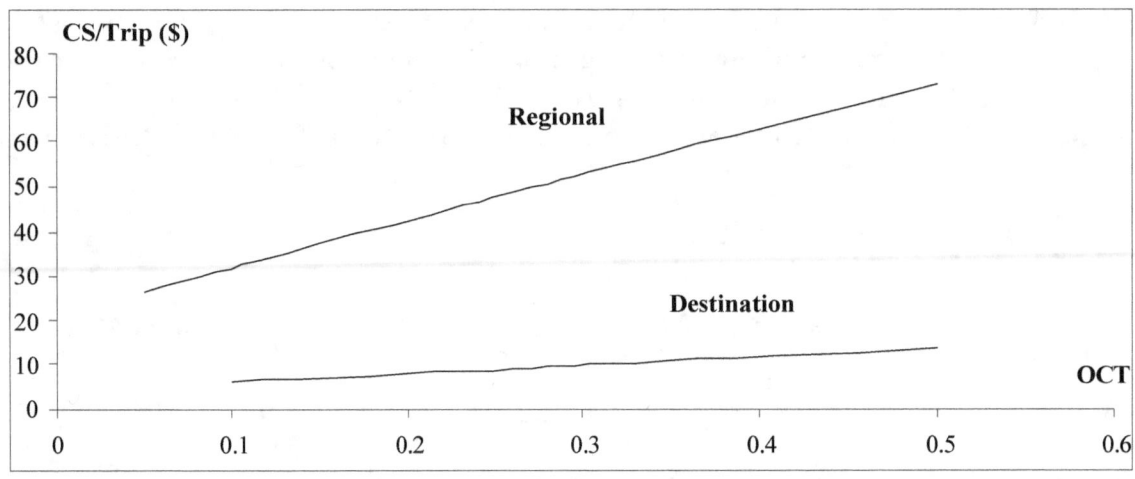

Figure 14:   *Variation of estimated consumer surplus per trip for both models.*

Of particular interest is that our preferred estimate of consumer surplus per trip is less than that estimated by Day (1987), although not by much. There are several differences in the way in which the two studies were conducted. These differences include the delineation of zones (concentric versus counties), the construction of the travel cost variable, the location and dates of surveys, among others. Probably the most important difference concerns the delineation of zones. Day (1987) constructed 10 zones covering states from Maine to Virginia. Travel costs from the more distant zones are likely to be substantial in the 1986 study, even after correcting for multiple site bias.[19] Holding other factors constant, higher levels of travel cost will lead to higher estimates of consumer surplus.

---

[19]Day (1987) handles the multiple site issue by surveying whalewatchers, as we did, about the importance of whalewatching relative to other vacation activities. As noted above, this approach could be a source of error because of the immediacy of the whalewatch activity relative to other activities. We also attempted to use the reported importance values to calculate estimates of travel cost. When the demand models were run, we discovered that travel cost had a positive coefficient, indicating an implausible upwardly sloping demand curve. The problem here is that reported importance values from most distant counties were fairly low. We would expect this to be the case because those who travel far are more likely to be doing other things in addition to whalewatching. Because participation rates were also low from those counties, we have a correlation between low participation and low (pro-rated) travel cost and vice versa.

Table 5: **Comparison of some consumer surplus estimates for recreation activities. All estimates are reported as per person per day or per trip and converted to 1996 dollars. Estimates may not be directly comparable due to differences in estimation methodologies.**

LOCATION/RECREATION ACTIVITY	ESTIMATED CS ($)	SOURCE
Visit to Old Orchard Beach, Maine	67	Lindsay and Tupper (1989)
Mean of 287 recreation valuation studies in the U.S. during 1968-88	38	Reported in Walsh et al. (1992)
Whalewatching from Gloucester, Massachusetts	33	Day (1987)
Whalewatching in New England	26	This report (1997)
Mean of 14 nonconsumptive fish and wildlife recreation valuation studies in the U.S. during 1968-88	25	Reported in Walsh et al (1992)
Access to a multispecies fishery in North Carolina (random utility model)	3	Kaoru (1991)
Creation of a new artificial reef fishing site in Florida	2-3	Milon (1988)

An important conclusion of this study is that a decision about what estimate is the more valid one relies on a modeling decision about how to handle the multiple site problem. In the Day (1986) study, the problem was handled by asking whalewatchers to state, in percentage terms, the importance of whalewatching to their trip. Then total travel costs were weighted by the reported percentage. We expect that polling whalewatchers on site about the importance of whalewatching to a vacation may result in overestimates of travel costs because of the immediacy (anticipation or satisfaction) of the activity in comparison to other vacation activities.   In this study, we assume away the multiple site issue by calculating travel costs for vacationers from the location of their vacation lodging. To do this, we are forced to accept some bias in the form of potentially nonrepresentative socioeconomic explanatory variables. This issue is illustrative of the difficulties involved in transferring estimates of benefits from one place and time to another.

REFERENCES

Bowes, M.D. and J.B. Loomis. 1980. A note on the use of travel cost models with unequal zonal populations. *Land Economics* 56(4): 465-470.

Bureau of the Census (BoC). 1996. Washington: U.S. Department of Commerce.

Day, S.V. 1987. Estimating the non-consumptive use value of whale watching: an application of the travel cost and contingent value techniques. Master's thesis. Kingston, R.I.: Department of Environmental and Natural Resource Economics, University of Rhode Island.

Department of Commerce and Department of the Interior (DoC and DoI). 1993. 1991 national survey of fishing, hunting, and wildlife-associated recreation. Washington (March).

Diamond, P.A. and J.A. Hausman. 1994. Contingent valuation: is some number better than no number? *Journal of Economic Perspectives* 8(4): 45-64.

Elasmar, M.G. 1996. A survey of attitudes toward whalewatching at Stellwagen Bank. Mimeo. Boston: Communications Research Center, Boston University.

Ellis, G.M. and A.C. Fisher. 1987. Valuing the environment as input *Journal of Environmental Management* 25: 149-156.

Freeman, A.M. 1996. The benefits of water quality improvements for marine recreation: a review of the empirical evidence. *Marine Resource Economics* 10: 385-406.

_____. 1993. *The Measurement of Environmental and Resource Values*. Washington: Resources for the Future, Inc.

Grandstaff, S. and J.A. Dixon. 1986. Evaluation of Lumpinee Public Park in Bangkok, Thailand. In J.A. Dixon and M.M. Hufschmidt, eds., *Economic Valuation Techniques for the Environment*. Baltimore, Md.: The Johns Hopkins University Press, pp. 121-140.

Hanemann, M. 1994. Valuing the environment through contingent valuation. *Journal of Economic Perspectives* 8(4): 19-44.

Hoagland, P. 1995. A methodological review of net benefit evaluation for marine reserves. Environment Department Paper No. 027. Washington: Pollution and Environmental Economics Division, Environment Department, The World Bank.

Hufschmidt, M.M. 1983. *Environment, Natural Systems and Development*. Baltimore: The Johns Hopkins University Press, pp. 216-232.

Kaoru, Y. 1993. Differentiating use and nonuse values for coastal water quality improvements. *Environmental and Resource Economics* 3: 487-494.

Lindsay, B.E. and H.C. Tupper. 1989. Demand for beach protection and use in Maine and New Hampshire: a contingent valuation approach. In O.T. Magoon et al., ed., *Proc. Of Coastal Zone '89.* New York: American Society of Civil Engineers, pp. 79-87.

McKean, J.R., D.M. Johnson and R.G. Walsh. 1995. Valuing time in travel cost demand analysis: an empirical investigation. *Land Economics* 71(1): 96-105.

Meeks, A. 1996. The whalewatching industry on Stellwagen Bank: an industry profile. Mimeo. Woods Hole, Mass.: Marine Policy Center, Woods Hole Oceanographic Institution.

Milon, J.W. 1988. A nested demand shares model of artificial marine habitat choice by sport anglers. *Marine Resource Economics* 5: 191-213.

National Agricultural Statistics Service (NASS). 1997. Cranberries. Washington: U.S. Department of Agriculture (19 August).

National Marine Fisheries Service (NMFS). 1997. Fisheries of the United States, 1996. Found at: http://remora.ssp.nmfs.gov/commercial/fus96/index.html.

_____. 1995. Marine recreational fisheries statistics survey. Silver Spring, Md.: National Oceanic and Atmospheric Administration.

New England Motor Rate Bureau (NEMRB). 1993. Tariff of highway mileages. Tariff NEB 119-D. Burlington, Mass.

Robert, A.P. 1997. Massachusetts travel industry stats2. Boston: Massachusetts Office of Travel and Tourism (6 June).

Sanctuaries and Reserves Division. 1993. Stellwagen Bank National Marine Sanctuary final environmental impact statement/management plan. Vols. I and II. Washington: NOAA, U.S. Department of Commerce (July).

Spatz, M.J., J.L. Anderson and S. Jancart. 1996. Northeast region aquaculture industry situation and outlook report: 1994-1995. Rhode Island Experiment Station Publication No. 3352. Kingston, R.I.: Department of Environmental and Natural Resource Economics, University of Rhode Island (June).

Terkla, D.G. 1990. Economic profile of Stellwagen Bank. In J.H. Archer, ed., *The Resources and Uses of Stellwagen Bank.* Boston: Urban Harbors Institute, pp. 23-31.

Walsh, R.G., D.M. Johnson and J.R. McKean. 1992. Benefit transfer of outdoor recreation demand studies, 1968-1988. *Water Resources Research* 28(3): 707-713.

www.ingramcontent.com/pod-product-compliance
Lightning Source LLC
Chambersburg PA
CBHW080426290526
45791CB00008BA/2416